Encounters
of a
Wayward Sailor

Encounters
of a
Wayward Sailor

TRISTAN JONES

SHERIDAN HOUSE

TO DARUMA

Daruma is a bearer of good fortune, revered in Japan. A Buddhist monk, he lost his legs after years of motionless meditation. Daruma dolls are fitted to weighted, rounded bases, and always roll upright when upset.

First published 1995 by
Sheridan House Inc.
145 Palisade Street
Dobbs Ferry, NY 10522

Copyright © 1995 by Sheridan House Inc.

Library of Congress Cataloging-in-Publication Data
Jones, Tristan, 1924-1995
    Encounters of a wayward sailor / Tristan Jones.
        p.   cm.
    ISBN 0-924486-80-5 (paperback: alk. paper)
    1. Jones, Tristan, 1924-1995 —Journeys.   2. Voyages and travels.
    I. Title.
    G465. J654 1995
    910. 4'5—dc20   95-35379
                                                              CIP

Editor: Janine Simon
Designer: Jeremiah B. Lighter

Printed in the United States of America

ISBN   0-924486-80-5

Foreword

Every reader cherishes a fantasy of meeting a beloved author. Few ever realize this dream except, perhaps, to shake the author's hand at a rushed and crowded bookstore autograph session. Yet, even such ephemeral encounters are forever replayed in our mind's eye as we lovingly recall the pressure of the hand, the smile of appreciation, the inflection of the voice, the two or three words uttered by our idol's lips, directed exclusively at us and no one else. We gaze and gaze and gaze at the inscription as if it were on the verge of quickening.

Imagine, then, what it must feel like to write a fan letter to an author and have him contact you to tell you he would like you to become his literary agent. But in fact, that is precisely how I came to represent Tristan Jones.

It happens that when I was younger I developed a passionate but totally incomprehensible love for books about the sea. I say incomprehensible because my only relationship to oceans has been to bathe in them. I have never taken an ocean voyage, am a lousy swimmer, have spent a total of two hours in sailboats, and my only attempt to learn sailing ended in a preposterous debacle when I snagged the keelboard of a rented Sunfish on the rope perimeter of a kiddie swim area in St. Thomas, capsized, and had to be rescued before a crowd of hundreds including my young son who up to that point considered me his hero.

Yet the lure of the sea, however vicariously satisfied in books, has held an immense power for me. I've read countless novels and true accounts of men locked in mortal combat against this most formidable of elements, and as a result of this obsession I daresay I can speak as knowledgeably about ships and sailing as any landbound man alive. Put me on the bridge of a British ship of the line and I *know* I could gain the wind over that clumsy tub of a galleon and blast her to the bottom of the Bay of Biscay.

It was this passion that led me to purchase Tristan Jones's original trilogy of seagoing adventures, *Saga of a Wayward*

Sailor, Ice!, and *The Incredible Voyage.* And it was the experience of immersing myself in his astonishing adventures, nar-
rated in his ravishing and lilting prose, that caused me to
write him a fan letter, in care of his publisher. You must understand that fan letters written by literary agents are not always as pure-hearted as billets-doux penned by the garden
variety of enamored readers. After expressing intense admira-
tion, such letters often end with a delicately worded expression of curiosity as to whether the author is—ahem—
represented by an agent. It is a matter of great pride for me
that my letter included no such solicitation. (All right, it *was*
written on my company letterhead.)

A few days later my secretary announced that Tristan
Jones was on the phone. I wondered from what exotic locale
this ship-to-shore communication came. The caller identified
his position as a pay phone at latitude Seventh Avenue, longitude 8th Street, in Greenwich Village on the sun-drenched isle
of Manhattan. My hero was a fifteen minute taxi ride from my
office! By the end of that fifteenth minute, he was sitting across
my desk from me. He told me that after selling his trilogy to
Andrews McMeel Publishers without benefit of representa-
tion, he had engaged a literary agent to handle subsequent
books. But he was no longer satisfied and had decided to seek
a new one. My letter had arrived at just the right time, and of
course, how could he not be represented by an agent who appreciated him so completely? We shook hands, and my fifteen
year voyage with Tristan Jones was launched. Naturally, as
with the launching of any other vessel, a bottle of spirits was
broken to celebrate, not over a boat's hull, but rather over two
glasses at a bar around the corner from my office.

Limitations of space prevent me from describing in detail
our relationship over the ensuing years. If you want to know
what Tristan did during that span of time, you need only to
read the accounts of his adventures that he published, many
of which are or will presently be available in Sheridan House
editions.

The volume you hold in your hands is a wide- and free-ranging account of Tristan's encounters with denizens both of the deep and of the earth's surface. He makes no bones about which species he respects more. All of his observations are infused with the patented Jones irony, the mordant wit of a survivor who long ago used up his government issue of lifetimes.

It was during my tenure as his agent that Tristan underwent the amputation of first one leg and then the other as a result of the slow deterioration of his limbs due to World War II injuries. I knew him to feel sorry for himself only once, after the first amputation. That emotion lasted only a few weeks before he concluded that self-pity was a stupid emotion, and his energy would be far better spent planning new voyages, mobilizing and motivating crews, and directing his literary agent to find the wherewithal to make it all happen.

It was my privilege to find the wherewithal to help finance some challenges that would daunt, and indeed had daunted, men possessed of two legs, including the conquest of a river that had never been navigated before, on a boat manned by a crew of handicapped youth. Those who scoffed at this mad scheme had mistakenly gazed at the stumps of Tristan's legs. They should have looked into his heart of oak, his will of carborundum steel, his irresistibly charming grin, and his resourceful mind of a million brilliant facets.

Tristan's correspondence with me over the course of our association is characterized by constant worry about money, by visions of new and improbable ventures, and by complaints: complaints about publishers, complaints about creditors, complaints about governments, complaints about everything and everybody including me. He was wise enough to complain only about things he could do something about, and to be stoical about those beyond his control. All of the former were eventually resolved, while the latter dissipated like storm clouds before Tristan's good-humored resignation. But there was one sorrow to which he never became reconciled: the failure of the world to recognize him in his time. It ate at his heart like a lamprey.

It ate at mine, too, and does to this day. I spent a great deal of time seeking ways to publicize Tristan's accomplishments in the media. But though he was (and still is) a legend in every port of call around the globe, honored by his peers of the Explorers Club, and celebrated by all who ply the seas in small crafts, the glory he deserves has never been accorded to him. It is nothing short of tragic that Tristan Jones, whose spirit is one with the likes of Burton, Speke, and Gordon, should not occupy a niche beside those immortals in the pantheon of human valor.

Tristan Jones died of a stroke on June 21, 1995. He had lived out his last years in a cottage in Phuket, Thailand, where he had rigged up a number of ingenious inventions for the accommodation of a legless sailor. He requested the following inscription on his tombstone:

TRISTAN JONES, SEAMAN, AUTHOR, AND EXPLORER
HE LOVED LIFE AND PAID HIS WAY

Also, in accordance with his will, Tristan's body was to be cremated, his ashes scattered at sea, "and a good bottle of dark rum poured after them." I am told that his last wishes were honored.

But it is for us the living to honor his most heartfelt wish: to keep his memory alive for future generations. We must not permit Tristan Jones to sink out of our consciousness "unknelled, uncoffined, and unknown."

RICHARD CURTIS
July 1995

Contents

PART

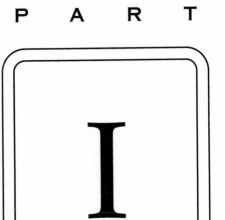

I

EPISODE 1

Ocean Voyaging

In 1953, for the first time I sailed alone. True, the first day of sailing there was little to do, which Andrew, the foreman at the boatbuilding yard, had told me. Nevertheless, on the first morning of departure as I let out the slack of the sheets, I had the deep thrill of having given life, or restored it, to my ship. Even though the yachts I delivered then and later were the property of others, when I was skipper and underway they were always "my ship."

My first delivery was a 38-foot sloop, *Alice B. Toklas*, from Holland direct to Barbados, where the lady owner would take her over and herself complete the voyage to her home port in Mexico.

My passage down the English Channel was all done on dead reckoning by taking note on the chart of notable coastal features passed. The same across the Bay of Biscay and down the Portuguese coast, to the Canaries. But from Gomera on, it was all ocean sailing. By that time the boat and I were used to each other.

As the island of Gomera dropped astern, *Alice B. Toklas'* black hull made deeply contented sounds as the sail filled, the great balloon curving voluptuously, a feminine sail if there ever was one. I had a sense of achievement far in excess of both cause and effect as she lunged forward heavily; she was too staid to leap. Sparkling stars of phosphorescence danced down the length of the hull until they met astern and burst together into a cloud of broken light.

I went aft and as the ship was steering herself well enough, the wheel having been lashed (no self-steering gear or auto-helms in those days), I was content to leave it so. The moment was too enjoyable to struggle and trim for the extra knot.

Sitting on the gunwale, I kept an eye on the compass and the sail, only hoping the latter would behave. I was free to walk the heaving deck, happy with our engineless motion, gloating in the company of our spinning log astern. The whole experience was so good that it could not have been broken down into comparisons without spilling some of the happiness. Perhaps it was the nearest I have been to ecstasy. My only regret was that I could not step aside and see *Alice B. Toklas* in all her newly revered beauty. Every time alone on that wide deck (it seemed wide at the time), that living piece of wood, was of immeasurable importance.

Back then, before self-steering gear was developed, if the wind was at all blustery, or calm, or shifting, I would sail single-handed only when I could stay awake. Otherwise I hove to, backing the staysail and hoisting a small trysail up the mast, so that my little ship stayed practically on the same spot until we resumed our course. It made for slower passages, but safer.

A gentle trade wind caressed our sails as we slipped mile after mile over a lazy ocean. Days were blue, intensely blue, with white, fleeting clouds. But the nights were sublime, unforgettable, with a crescent moon and flickering phosphorescent lights on the horizon. One night, with a soft thud, *Alice B. Toklas* touched some great fish—perhaps a sleeping whale.

We had no electronic weatherfaxes then. Those first ocean-sailing days I was as close to nature as I'll ever get. I began to rely on instinct as to what the day had in store. I noted the shape and direction of the clouds, and connected them with the weather conditions. The yacht was always creaking and groaning and I soon knew all the different sounds: the slapping as a halyard slackened, the knock of the tiller-rope worked loose, the grinding of the whisker pole as it slipped from its proper position on the mast, the knocking of something adrift in the cabin.

So smoothly did the days flow by in *Alice B. Toklas* that there was little to report . . . unless something out of the ordinary occurred. I wrote up the log only once a day, after plotting my noon position. When the trade wind was steady, the ship steered herself. Below it was comfortable and, with the companionway closed, surprisingly quiet. Only, at the start of the trans-ocean voyage, a ham swinging in the galley thudded against the bulkhead and pots and pans clinked in the locker. I soon got things shipshape and noiseless. A sea occasionally breaking under the counter astern yawed the ship and rumbled beneath the bilge. The water racing by the oak planking only a foot from my ear was the music of a fast passage that brought contented sleep. When I sailed at night it was beautiful beyond description and I ached to prolong the moments into eternity.

So my voyage went; each day of twenty-four hours a little step forward, a dot beyond the last. I seemed always to know the position of the boat, and I saw her moving across the chart, which became a picture before me. We would cut a path just a dozen or so feet wide across the ocean, like a meteor wandering through the solar system.

I got the boat into regular and comfortable weather and a one knot westward-helping stream in the North Equatorial Current, and myself into that routine of sea life which is broken only by storm, another sail in sight (very rare in those days), or the loom of land.

The nights were crowded wonders of stars; the dawns always a promise. *Alice B. Toklas* went easy, as the sea was easy. There was just enough of a following wind, one time for four days, dead easterly it was, to keep her steady and the boom square in its right place out alee, nor did it shake or swing as boats so often will before a following sea, but went on with a purpose. So she sailed and astern we left a little bubbling wake, which in the darkness had glimmered with evanescent and magic fires, but now, as the morning broadened, could be seen to be white foam. The stars paled for an hour and then soon vanished, and although the sun had not yet risen, it was day.

Then followed days of supreme sailing. The seas piled up on our quarter and we slithered from one white-topped sapphire ridge to the next, driving her to the limit under mainsail and a small spinnaker. I would turn in for four hours' rest at seven o'clock in the evening. Then I would stay at the helm until four in the morning, then turn in for another four hours. And so it went. Sometimes if the wind was steady I would let her steer herself. Then, down below, absorbed in trying to identify the various creakings and galley noises that blended with the rushing sound of the sea on the other side of the one-inch planking, I would fall asleep.

Now, slowly but surely the mark of my little ship's course on the track-chart reached out on the ocean and across it, while at her utmost speed she marked with her keel still slowly the sea that carried her. So the little dots which represented our noon positions advanced over the tracking chart, while the sea and the sky remained to all intents and purposes unchanged. But as the only indications of progress, these dots, however unreal their message, always received my keenest attention.

I thought of the hours I'd spent planning this voyage back in Holland. At the point of an indomitable lead pencil I had traversed vast tracks of ocean in the twinkling of an eye, and explored the furthermost corners of the earth, and if there is a more fascinating evening's entertainment, I should like to hear of it. Rather hazily, each day, I had considered the width of this ocean. Maps and charts make for a sophisticated regard for the wide expanses of the earth, until an entire ocean may be visualized as a few inches on the surface of a map.

Nowadays, ashore, TV seems to have all but made the oceans disappear, except for "environmental" programs or shipping disasters. Now, just about everyone has information on the oceans, but comparatively few *know* about them; information and knowledge are two vastly different things.

Back to 1953, *Alice B. Toklas* and the chart: suddenly for the first time, I awoke to the full realization of the enormity of the task ahead of me. *Infinity*, the old familiar term of school geometry lessons, took on a concrete meaning. It was *the distance to Barbados*.

I looked over the chart and began to feel horribly microscopic and unimportant and very far from home. It seemed quite impossible that I had come so far. The thousands of miles that lay far ahead often appear insuperable. Distance lends them an aura of awe. But as the voyage progresses, each step is studied and accomplished as an independent chore. Before you realize it, you have succeeded in completing what seemed originally a colossal undertaking; not by one long-sustained effort, but rather by a connected series of short efforts, each one a complete whole. I scaled down the distances from miles to feet, and on this particular passage my ship was seen as but a grain of dust blown slowly over a half-mile plane, a fleck of dust that can cover little more than a hundred feet from sun-up to sun-up.

Then a full gale blew. All that day, *Alice B. Toklas* raced dead west before the wind, baring her black boot top, climbing and planing with intense effort, her sails curved and gripping the wind as the cotton raked stiff-bunted under the glowing sky. Sunset and she continued to sweep down miles, lurching into the night, which made the swing of the sea appear as a rush of green and bronze, with scattered crests, rolling brass-headed, flaming in hazy light. *Alice B. Toklas'* bows gashed the living sea, her entire hull bottom thundered. And in the morning, I was still grimly hanging on to the tiller and she was still storming onwards, straining, overeager, a flash of wake screwing astern in the early sunshine, her mainsail skintight and biting at the backstays. Noon found me sextant in hand, taking a last noon sight before landfall on Barbados. She was still moving, and I held her with a stiff helm.

West! It is curious how the land comes up from the sea after a passage of many days across open ocean, a passage the progress of which has been measured until then only upon a chart with penciled lines calculated from much observing of the sun, the moon and the stars, and the working of involved trigonometrical formulae simplified by tables. Slowly the lines on the chart had headed towards the darkened landmass of Barbados on its left hand corner, and for a long time there was nothing but the lengthening lines and water, water, water, which might always be the same, in the same place, only behaving differently, varying in its deceits and its moods.

Now, each noon, when I laid down my latitude, I would ask myself, "How much further to Barbados?" And I would carefully measure from the little cross on the chart in miles, then roughly convert the miles into hours, and hours into literature, and answer myself: "One Oxford Book of English Poetry, one novel by Conrad, one Conan Doyle story." Finally, when Barbados hovered on the horizon, pale and ghostly blue, I started the motor.

Take with a pinch of salt anything told you by anyone who claimed he or she was an expert "celestial navigator," at least in yachts. On such unstable platforms as small craft underway, celestial navigation, using a sextant, was never an easy task, and neither was the result often accurate. There was little expertise but an awful lot of luck. We used to kid ourselves that we were experts and that for us it was easy, but we were wrong. Each sextant session was a fussy project, with each result, unless land was in sight, in doubt, as to accuracy of instrument, timing or angle. Over many parts of all oceans there were radio blind spots, where time signals could not be obtained. We still relied on chronometers, and these could be anything up to several minutes in error.

On one occasion, many years later, while navigating in

the Red Sea, I had found myself, according to my celestial calculations of longitude, to be within the (forbidden to infidels)
walled city of Mecca. This error was probably due to the heat
of the sun causing intense evaporation from the coral reefs
which extend way out into the sea, and so causing undue re-
fraction. Even dead-reckoning should not be relied on too
much. Once, on a foggy day in Long Island Sound, I found my
boat supposedly, according to my chart and a street-map of
New York City, sitting on top of a skyscraper on the West Side
of Manhattan.

When the time came to take a sight of some celestial body
or other, you opened your sextant case, and invariably wondered at how beautiful both the case and the instrument inside it had been made. How intricate it was, with its bright arc
so cleanly and minutely graduated. Once or twice, in a crewed
yacht, you might see, oxidized on the silver, someone else's
thumbprint, and know that curiosity had been afoot. But not
even for that would you polish the sextant arc; the stain of the
thumbprint would less obscure the graduations of the arc
than the erosion of polishing. Then you would carefully clamber topside with the sextant case held like the Holy Grail. You
would find a safe place to set down the case. You would take
your sextant in hand, twist your legs around the halyards or
stays, brace your shoulders between them, and resting one
eye as it were on that fixed point of the absolute, the sun, and
the other on the immutable horizon of this earth, find by tri-
angulation "where I am."

Navigation under sail, using the Pilot books (based on the
work of men long gone) and sextant, does strange things to
one's view of the world. It is not merely a method of finding
one's way—it is an extension of our minds into the heavens,
and an extension of our minds into the past, so that for a while
we are contemporaries of the long dead. The long night-
watches alone are eminently adapted to draw out the reflec-
tive faculties. No one who does not comprehend and

appreciate these facts can ever understand the mind of an ocean sailor.

Then one day from the whited chart and from the water the land stands up. It *was* there. It has not only its existence in the dark outlines on the chart; it is a different land from that we left. It is the land to which we have been *bound*.

That Barbados had appeared where it should and when it should, caused me, even to myself, to endeavor to conceal my surprise under a mask of indifference, implying that I had never seriously doubted the reliability of my navigation. But deep down I knew the truth: all that had allowed any reliability to my navigation and safe arrival was God, the boat builders, the weather, and a great big chunk of luck.

I don't recall any special feeling of triumph on my first trans-oceanic landfall. I'm pretty certain, though, that I wouldn't have felt as satisfied as I did if I'd been merely pushing buttons to find out where I was.

In Barbados, the lady-owner and her two women crew took over *Alice B. Toklas* alright, very capably, too. She was a generous soul. After feting me royally around Kingstown, she presented me with a nice fat tip. Unfortunately her boat never made it home to Mexico. Off Belize she was wrecked in a hurricane. The lady and her crew, however, somehow survived.

EPISODE 2

Sunsets and Storms

When I think of the surroundings of the ocean sailor, all the variety, my mind boggles. He sees things that most city-dwellers can only dream of. Dawns which come up with fiery red splashes over seas of nickel, skies clear except for a solitary gun puff of cloud, seas crinkled silver, water as unfathomable, to us simpler souls, as the black holes between the stars at night.

I remember times in the northern latitudes when the wan and sickly daylight lasted a bare three hours, sometimes less, out of the twenty-four. For the rest of the time I was plunged into complete darkness, a cold, hail smitten darkness, black as the Earl of Hell's riding boots. Then there were times when the wind, having gone by dawn, left behind it a damp, sniveling day, brightening and darkening with hysterical indecision and always on the edge of tears. There were the clear, cold skies overhead that looked like a steel blue cymbal that might ring should you smite it. How I recall those clear blue skies in the moderate latitudes. Off Cornwall, where, with the sun high overhead in summer, there would be a fresh edge to the air, a hint of an approaching autumn and time to head off south. The sky was a hard, cloudless blue, and the coast and the inland hills stood out in sharp scraped lines.

Surroundings during calm weather in northern climes were remarkable, too. Often the diffused light of the short daybreak showed the open water to the south-westward, sleeping, smooth and gray under a faded heaven. Sometimes hailstones rattled on deck like piles of dried peas. Overhead a gray sloppy sky, around me a gray, sloppy sea. The rocky high coast threw a heavy belt of gloom along the inshore shoals, which, in the calm of expiring light, were unmarked by the slightest ripple. As I stared at the scene, I would reflect to myself that far away outside this gloomy region, under some legendary clear sky, the sun was setting. My sun rose with a wan and spectral glare in which I expected to see some haunted cosmic face gazing sightlessly over the sea, whispering a doom through metal lips.

All I got was thunder and a sudden gush of rain.

Sunsets I find impressive, but sunrises even more beautiful. To me, sunrise over a tropical sea is the most glorious sight on God's earth. But it's too common an occurrence. If it happened only, say, once a year, travelers would come from all over the globe to marvel at it. To see in a few moments the velvety blackness of night tremble through veils of paling purple, hueless gray, and all shades of azure, delicate rose, and flashing gold to the imperial blaze of the rising sun is an unforgettable experience. Sunrise anywhere is a glorious sight, but it puts on its most ineffable beauty at sea between the Tropics of Cancer and Capricorn. Looking at it I feel the same sort of illumination as the prophet of old when he exclaimed "God is light!"

In the days before dependable radio or TV weather forecasts, when things like onboard weatherfaxes would have been looked upon as the wildest dreams of a mad professor, I often used to sail with clever, knowledgeable people who would take one look at the sky at dawn and say "Hmm, I don't like the look of the sky this morning. We shall have a strong wind today." The ominous signs which were so visible to them were invisible to me, so I used to go below, tap my barometer glass and wonder whether they were right. But often as not they were wrong.

In the more southerly latitudes, and on ocean passages, I

learned to read the sky like a map. All over the sky the little trade-wind clouds were scattered evenly. There was no break in the pattern until I came nearer to a high island. Then over the island there would be a mount of cumulus, like a sheep in a field of lambs.

The island would be passed, or arrived at and departed, and it would drop astern and disappear. Then there would be what seemed to be a special display for my boat and for me: a minute speck in the vastness of sky and water. As soon as the fiery sun dipped below the horizon, the western sky turned peach-colored, then orange, and finally a deep rich red. At the same time, the sky changed from duck-egg blue to indigo velvet as night came stealing across from the east. The glow in the west faded like red-hot iron cooling. It was all over by seven o'clock, a warning that long nights were ahead.

One sunset I remember just east of the Marquesas was almost beyond words to describe. The sun had scarcely set when the whole western half of the sky became pink, then a rose, then a ruby red. The undersides of a few clouds radiated like fire across the sky. The topsides in contrast were a deep valley of charcoal black. It looked as though the entire sky had caught aflame. The scene lasted fully five minutes before it faded. The glow went out in the uppermost clouds, then the lower clouds, and the horizon dimmed as the color burned away, leaving the sky ashen gray with puffs of charcoal here and there.

Tropical thunderstorms, with their splendid lightning displays, always remind me of a time in the Cape Verde Islands. I was making my way into a remote bay to anchor. I was standing in the stern of this schooner I was delivering to Brazil. I was holding on to the backstays, sighting into the pitch-black night, with the compass bowl between my feet, when there was a blistering flash of lightning that showed me the very limpets clinging to the rocks of the northern arm of the bay . . .

The Western Caribbean probably has more lightning and varieties of clouds than anywhere else. The spawning ground of most of the clouds that pass over the eastern United States, eastern Canada and Britain is off the south coast of Cuba. There, off the coasts of Honduras or Mexico, the squall clouds march down from the eastern horizon like a disorganized army fleeing the enemy, and a larger mass of them might have as many as a dozen tentacles groping towards the sea, ranging from little ice-cream cones to full-fledged vortices that draw the sea up into the body of the cloud and roar out the challenge of their short existences. It can be a frightening place to be in a small craft, especially at night, when as many as a hundred lightning flashes at a time can make the idea of Hades pale. There might be a pause around midnight, but then the horrible outbursts would continue, fiercer apparently, and more fiendish than ever. At times the whole sky would be a dense cobweb of lightning, flooding every crack and corner with an abominable brightness that seemed to intrude into even the deepest crevasses of my soul. Then again, in the blackness that followed, my boat would be rushing through wide streaks of dully glowing water, which stood out sharply, without surroundings, without background, like a flood of luminous milk in a vacuum. What it was, I could not tell. Perhaps the phosphorescence caused by billions of microscopic beings, isolated by meeting currents. Perhaps only one more among many weird electrical phenomena, which add to the indescribable horror of some nights off the east coast of Central America. What it must have seemed like to the first European sailors to reach here, in all their superstitions, is far beyond my imagination to even wonder.

But not all cloud cradles are like hell. Often I have sat in my cockpit off some high tropical island and watched the birth of fair-weather cumulus. A light haze would begin to lift out of a valley and, as it drifted, a mist which had been hanging over a nearby hillside would slide towards it. An unseen dip in the hill would discharge, like a gun puff, a small cloud of what seemed to be smoke. The land was beginning to warm and soon every bank and fold and cave were firing white shells into the air. The cloud would thicken and darken. The wind would blow it sideways and, as it rose, it would topple into the shape of an old man's head. After an hour or so it was full-grown, and it would drift inland to join other morning clouds.

The following day I might be twenty miles from the island, and see the self-same cloud, now a mass all across the sky, come bowling up from the horizon, messengers, outriders, or comrades of the coming gale.

Far more dangerous to mariners than typhoons or hurricanes are fogs. Without radar (as not so long ago we all were), fog is the most bewildering difficulty of the many to be encountered at sea in a small craft. I was once asked by an estimable old gentleman who accompanied me from Colombia to Aruba in *Outward Leg*, in the middle of a raging gale which we were bucking heavily to windward to make our easting for Willemstad, if "the weather got any worse than this?" The question took me so flat aback I hadn't the wits to tell him that for a sailing boat it couldn't get any better. The same old gentleman rejoined me for two days much later when *Outward Leg* reached the English Channel. He slept peacefully in his bunk when we ran into thick fog and slowed down to about six knots ("Ollie" was a trimaran and fast). He would probably have been surprised to learn that he was in more danger then than he'd ever been off the coast of Colombia.

Six miles southeast of the Needles, at the western end of the Isle of Wight, *Outward Leg* was creeping along under power, feeling her way down vistas of eddying fog-smoke, when we heard a pulsing throb and low swish of water. I grabbed the fog alarm and pressed the trigger. A toot dissipated into the smoke fog. Suddenly a giant shape loomed up out of the thickness of the mist, seeming to drop down on top of us. There was no time to do anything, the ship was almost

into us. It was touch and go; only a few yards separated the
vessels, when there was a clatter of bells onboard the ship and
she swerved sharply to port. She missed our stern by only a
few feet, traveling at about 25 knots. For a moment, she tow-
ered up like some colossal wraith of the sea, then melted
rapidly into the mist. But that did not leave us at all safe, until
three hours later, when the fog finally lifted. Even then we still
had something like fifty ships an hour passing us.

For of all creatures of Gaia, the sea is the most various. We
should not blame the sea for its moods or perils. The sea asks
for nothing but to be left alone, and lies there and would be
forever at peace if it were not for sundry bullies, the moon
pulling, the sun hauling, and the waters frozen and melted
and heated and evaporated and condensed, and swung round
continents and capes by the sun and the moon, and over
shoals and reefs and the air charging down angrily and dis-
turbing all, till the sea cannot call its soul its own. Then, on top
of all that, we have people now rushing all over the sea and
into its deepest depths, killing its creatures, stealing its greatest treasures. No wonder if the sea gets a touch of anger now
and then and takes a few human lives.

There comes a moment when a sailor realizes that it is not
the wind that is his opponent in the Greatest Game of All, but
the sea. In all his struggles he has fought, he thinks, with the
power and fury of the wind, and even perhaps found exhilaration in the roar of a great gale ringing and shrieking in the
rigging. For years, until this truth comes home, he thinks that
he has dealt with the wind, that the "wrestle with natural
forces" has been against the wind, with the wind, to master it,
to control it. Nothing can be further from the truth. The struggle is with the sea.

There will come a time when the wind is blowing hard
enough, yet there will be no sense that it is the enemy. The real
enemy will be seen clearly enough then: seething, leaping and
appalling water so close. All that chaotic water of tumult is the

enemy; always alert and on the clutch and on the pounce. Devils will surge up from it and fling their fingers onto the deck, and the teeth of other devils will flash out at the rudder and the keel and into the cockpit. And the teeth of those devils will make all the wealth, all the goods, all the physical properties that are valued by humanity seem *tawdry*. As far as the eye will see there will be a dimness of tossing, drab, angry devils with grabbing and gleaming tusks and claws, with drift cut off sharp from the tops of the seas and flung flat with the scooped scud; with strange sheers and scurries and dives and glides in the yacht, which will somehow seem to find her own way, guided by your hand—you, the savage at the helm—and you will be aware of nothing but the nakedness of your soul pitted against a savagery you could only once start to imagine.

Then there will be a strain on the leaning shoulder of your white darkened sail, then a pause, then a seething of white along your gunwale and a slashing of more spray, and curses from you, and eventually, when you know you have not won, but survived, you will render your thanks to God for your self-draining cockpit and your modern materials.

I think of the weather I have come through. How in the Indian Ocean, off dangerous Cape Gardafui, I carried a jib and mizzen only for a week solid, and how *Barbara* buried her deck steadily and groaned and labored like a thing in agony. Hove down so far by the force of the wind and sea she took those crushing blows on her sweetly shaped hull where they lost their destructive force. That gale ended as suddenly as it had started. Just about sunrise on the seventh day we got for an hour an inexplicable steady breeze right in our teeth. There was no sense to it. It fitted neither the season of the year nor the experience of seamen as recorded in the Pilot books, nor the aspect of the sky. Only purposeful malevolence could account for it. It sent us traveling eastwards at a great pace away from our proper course, which was south, and if we had been out on a pleasure sail it would have been a delightful breeze, with an awakened sparkle in the sea, with the sense of motion, and a feeling all around of undeserved freshness. Then all at once, as if disdaining to play with us further, it dropped and died out completely in less than five minutes. The boat's head swung where it wanted; the stilled sea took on the polish of a steel plate.

Storms return to my memory time and again. I recall once, in mid-Atlantic, bound for the Azores from Newport, waiting for a storm. I'd heard a vague warning to shipping over the BBC radio, but that had been for areas farther east than I was. Now, out of the darkness of the storm ahead such a sea was lifting as I had never seen. The first sight of it was to me as though a low range of hills was moving bodily forward; then the effect changed in my mind to that of a line of crags. It was dark, toothy at the top with fangs, like the body of the night below, and was moving with a life of its own from some-where I could not even begin to imagine. All at once I had the dreadful feeling that it was alive. How high it was I could not guess, but higher certainly than any wave I had ever previ-ously seen. It seemed, to me, not like a wave; it was *Judgment Day* advancing, wolfing up all the sea into its power and lick-ing out the sky with its tongue. I could only gasp to myself: "My God, that's it." I did not doubt for one second as the thing approached that it was for me the end. It seemed indeed to be more likely the end of the world.

Of course, it wasn't the end. But my goodness what a drubbing!

Gales and Calms

Keeping sails whole and sound was a painstaking chore which went on forever before the days of man-made fiber sails. Then, in the 50s and early 60s, sails, at least for European yachts, were mainly of canvas, flax or cotton. I can't begin to count the number of hours I've spent at sea repairing torn sails. It must run into the hundreds, if not thousands, of hours. Once, I left Fowey in England, and within twenty minutes of sailing out of the harbor a squall struck my cutter and tore to ribbons the staysail that I had worked on to repair for ten solid hours only the two days before. It was gone quicker than you could say "Ease!"

Gales are nothing to smirk or drivel over; and the smaller your boat is, down to a certain limit, the better your chance of coming through a storm unharmed. Although the sea builds up into mighty mountains, the waves move in steady processions, and you can easily make your way through the chop that rides them. But in a hurricane, the wind not only blows with a force sufficient to rip metal fittings from their housings, but the sea comes from all directions in a smother that could swamp even the tightest boat, unless hatchboards are in place.

The sea, the ocean, in all its forceful majesty is something not easily forgotten. I recall an evening glance to windward under a waxing moon. My boat *Arusha* was well into mid-Atlantic on a passage from New York to Plymouth, England.

As I say, I looked to windward and saw a black shape reared from horizon to horizon. As *Arusha* dropped down the slope, I knew we were fated to meet the greatest sea I had ever come upon until that time. We climbed again and I caught sight of its long moving body, already much nearer. This time as my boat dropped down, my heart sank with her. She was surely too small, too thin, for the purpose. I watched the inflexible purpose, the unfaltering purpose, of the wave, that now gleamed in one moonlit plane, now darkened into heaving shadow, disappeared, lifted again, and rolled on and down towards us. Then suddenly the wave was beyond and *Arusha* was victoriously sinking to the trough. Glancing fearfully, yet relieved, over my shoulder, I looked up to a receding form inclining in a tremendous slide of dragging foam to a crest, windy, shining. Already a quarter of a mile away, it made a freakish lunge towards the sky, tumbled, dropped into a smooth fall, and with infinite majesty glided into oblivion. That huge sea had proved itself a "fair-weather wave," as we sailors say. It marked the height of the storm, and forecasted the coming of less boisterous weather.

Again in a night watch, in the 40-foot Dutch yawl *Slot Van Keppel* in the Southern Ocean, I recall how there was suddenly a sound in the gloom that by now we knew only too well; a sound somewhere between the immense whisper a big sea makes as it prepares to turn over, and the cracking roar as it does. I groped hurriedly for something to hold onto as we jerked around to peer astern with wide and wary eyes. Against the faintest silver of the southeastern sky an Andean ridge of black water was marching hugely at dawn. It was one of those big seas that travel alone; a rogue elephant of the ocean. Its massive head was swaying and tossing with a leisurely deliberation that spoke imperiously to some primitive center in us. And *Slot* was already soaring up its black precipitous face. As its impending head leaned over, she increased her efforts to mount it. With a creaking groan from all her gear, she leapt again into the darkness and reached the ridge. For a breathless moment, as we were carried forward in a flurry of the wind, we could see the black depth from which we had climbed and, on the other side, to which we should presently sink. We could also look out over a boundless waste of shouldering seas, their bases as black as the night, their heads all silvered in the frigid light of the dawn. Then *Slot*'s stern dipped steeply; her bowsprit pointed wildly at the paling heavens, and, as she floated dizzily down to the hollow, there was a shattering roar. The mountainous sea broke ahead of her, and thundered away on its passage to the horizon, leaving behind it an acre of dulling foam. Into this field of moon-flowers which had magically bloomed in the darkness, *Slot* lurched wearily, and was surrounded by a fierce hissing of millions of bursting bubbles. In the gloom my own voice exclaimed, "Thank God there's not an 80-knot wind behind that little lot!"

But all was not over. For a few seconds we lay, as it were, stricken and faint. Another white-lipped monster was rolling up astern, but before it reached us *Slot* seemed to make a mighty effort. She quivered and labored heavily up, throwing the water from her deck and lifting her streaming bows. As the roller swung down on us, her stern rose slowly to it, and it surged on and under, lifting Slot on its shoulders, spouting cataracts from every gunwale port. So it went on, day after day, *for eighteen days and nights in a row*.

But sooner or later the light always comes up at dawn. Far over the sea, the shapes of running swells were passing in slow procession across the red hot-glowing face of the rising sun with massive deliberation and indescribable delicacy throwing their shadows afar. A gigantic peristalsis of the sea over the burning body of the sun; a hidden function of the darkness just passed secret and withheld was suddenly revealed by the coming of the day. Feathered clouds seen in long, closing perspective gathered over the sun in a marbled arm. Beneath the opulence of their ranks, the sea, strangely without color, spread an endless ice-blue vista over which the swells were marching in legions, each bearing a cresset of cold fire.

Then the polar winds. There's something to remember with icicles in my heart. One "day" (it was as dusky as evening) an 80-knot wind, sweeping down from the ice fields of East Greenland, blew in my face, freezing and crying. The sky was naked, almost blue—a dirty blue—and near its zenith a last-quarter moon shone light onto the crests of black waves, of waves traveling at high speed, now resembling tall cliffs rather than mountains, cliffs formed by the cutlass slashes of wind, ripped into storm patterns, now of a solid unforgiving black, now glowing in great fissures of infuriated silver, and sounding iron-like above the roaring wind. My back was to the bows of *Cresswell*, away from her mainmast that resembled a stunted arm raised against the awful night. I saw only the tiny, whale-backed afterdeck, the surface protrusions picked out by the moon, beaded with frozen water, the stiff parts of ropes, wet and shining, on the narrow deck. That's Arctic sailing. But it was not the most frightening.

To face the elements is, to be sure, no small undertaking when the sea is in its grandest mood. You must know the sea, and know that you know it, and bear in mind that it is made to be sailed over. But you must also know your boat, and her purpose, even more. For weeks on that voyage I was never sure of the sea; I was always uncertain whether it would show itself a friend or an enemy in the intimate proximity I myself sought. When swallowed up in the darkness, I heard a general noise from the sea suddenly deafened by the hiss of a roller close by and saw a white crest come groping towards me on a level with my cabin roof. I held on tight and waited uneasily to feel the masses of water smash down on *Slot* and the raft lashed to her foredeck. But every time there was the same surprise and relief. *Slot* swung up her stern and rose skyward unperturbed, while the masses of water rolled along her sides.

And so I learned to trust—not the sea, but the boat.

On one particular night, way, way out in the middle reaches of the South Atlantic, in the midst of the doldrums, there was no wind. Sea-wise, that was the most fearful time of them all. *Slot*, under her slowly swaying mast, in a glittering stillness, was waiting for a wind. In the evening all was quiet, no wind, flat sea. Suddenly I heard a distant roar of breaking water. It rapidly got louder and nearer; I lowered all sail and stood by waiting for the worst. Soon I could make out the phosphorescent gleam from broken wave crests astern, and in a moment or two they were all around. *Slot* jumped and tossed about, the waves broke aboard. The roar passed away, the sea became calm, and so did I. The whole time, there had not been a breath of wind.

My little tale will show you how far ocean yachting has come in a mere forty years. For some days at a time the doldrums had *Slot* in its grip. You must bear in mind that in those engineless days to be becalmed was a fearful experience, to watch your water and food slowly and steadily diminish, and to make no headway. *Slot* lay helpless on an oily sea, her mast sticking up idly into the still air. The heat grew terrific; bare metal was too hot to touch and the pitch bubbled out of the seams between the deck-planking and stuck to my bare feet. The flax and cotton sails were all stowed below to save their rotting in the sun. Every time there was a breath of a breeze I would haul the light cotton mainsail up on deck, clap it on the parrels and hoist it aloft. There it would uselessly flop. Then I would hear the grasp and grind of the parrels as the boat rocked to some imperceptible swell.

It was exasperating. My freshwater tanks were almost empty; I was down to a ration of a quarter of a pint a day. The cockpit was like a furnace and my only amusement was to scan the face of the heavens and whistle for a wind.

After twenty-two days of being utterly becalmed, the sky became overcast, a black thundercloud overspread everything, and then, without a warning, down came the deluge. I shouted for joy. I ran naked over the deck and writhed under the downpour in the rapidly-filling cockpit (no self-draining in those days). The clouds seemed to collapse, the rain fell in sheets and torrents with such intensity it was impossible to see more than a few yards, and the sea gave off a continual hissing roar under the violence of the downpour. With a spasmodic rattle of heavy drops on deck, the rain swished away with a great sigh of relief over the sea.

Then, as suddenly as it began, the rain stopped, the clouds rolled away, and the sun shone down again with undiminished vehemence upon my drenched and steaming boat.

But my fresh-water tanks were almost full again.

Waterspouts are another thing. When you see a squall with dark fingers, and when those fingers are working, it's time to hand sail. But sometimes there's no warning, and this is often the case with waterspouts. Their main breeding ground, the most prolific, is the western Caribbean.

I was off the Costa Rican coast, making my way down to Panama in a 40-foot sloop, *Go Getter*. All was steady and I had a self-steering gear working. I sat below at my cabin table working out my noon position. I suddenly had a strange feeling that something was amiss. A glance up through the companionway quickly changed my uneasiness to alarm, for there, directly astern and catching up with *Go Getter* rapidly, still in the first throws of birth, hung the biggest waterspout I had ever clapped eyes on. Its long black tentacle, suspended from the lowering, tumultuous mother cloud, writhed and groped halfway to the sea, like the arm of a giant octopus seeking a grip on a victim.

My eyes clung to it fascinated as it reached down and down, sometimes retreating but always growing again. Then I heard the distant roaring of a sighing sound, that reminded me of a waterfall heard from a distance. Underneath the spout, at the surface of the sea, the sympathetic disturbance suddenly became more intense, as the incipient whirl revolved faster and faster, throwing off bits of foam and loose water. A distinct bulge in the surface appeared, as if sucked up by the thirsty column above, and rode higher every second. The spray and foam now began to be snatched upward and before my eyes was formed a watery connection with the descending tube, linking cloud and sea. The base grew larger and more violent as it received the too-heavy particles thrown away from the column by centrifugal force. The noise and tumult grew as the hissing of the column, the scream of the wind, and the crashing of the waters blended into a fearsome roar. Augmented by more and more water, the lower half suddenly reached maturity and groped out to clasp hands with the upper half, and the sea and the sky were united in a spinning, weaving pillar of water.

Weather, a simple and unpretentious but nevertheless basic element, is, like some kinds of food, spurned by those who can easily avoid it, but at sea its power, and above all its omnipresence, command an awed respect. To landspeople watching TV from their sofas, it is a series of squiggles on a map and a pointer wielded by a handsome or beautiful person, and becomes something again convenient or avoidable, as required by the viewer; something not quite real. Ashore, the natural forces must work themselves into a typhoon, an earthquake, a monstrous flood, to gain due attention and adulation, but on the ocean the weather's every whim is reflected by its sycophant, the sea. But all on the ocean is not risk and gloom. For days the weather may vary between full storm and light gale; the sea will dig itself up into wide valleys filled with the smoke from foaming gray-blue seas, which will seem to have their backs pressed out long and flat under the onset of the wind. But then, sooner or later, the heavens will split open to reveal a glimpse of blue, and the malignant black cloud cover will give way to a victorious blue sky as the storm passes on. Nobody has ever found a substitute for the sweet chuckling of water, like the laughter of water-babies, that you hear outside the hull while lying in a small yacht's bunk. Nobody has ever found a substitute for the pure natural joy of sailing on a clear sunny day: how the waves meet her bows, to dash them into myriads of sparkling gems that hang about her at every surge.

The day will be perfect, the sunlight clear and strong. Popcorn-like frills of wavelets will appear everywhere on the tops of swells. The roaring seas, which for a day or two have jumped up and glared at you, will have turned into gossiping waves that ripple and patter against your boat's sides as she rolls along among them, delighted with their story. The waves will doff their white caps beautifully to her before the steady wind.

You will look to windward and see the sea still tumbling, and a great number of white waves. Your heart will be so high that you will give names to the waves: the long-haired wave, the graceful wave, the wave that will break on the beach of a beautiful island a long way off, the wave that brings good tidings, the wave that will run round and round the world and never stop until the end of time itself. And smaller seas will fall and climb onto the backs of their parents.

And as the wind eases more, some of the seas will get out of control, becoming as if crazy, and tower up into a huge pyramid and break quite unpredictably. Every particle of water thrown into the air will become a gem, and the boat, pounding ahead, will snatch necklace after necklace from the sea, and as often throw them away. We have all seen miniature rainbows about a tug's bow, but when your boat flings out her own they will be such as you have never seen before. You will know then that your boat's good angel has embarked her on her voyage; you will read it into the sea.

EPISODE 4

Some Anchorages

I suppose one of the most wacky anchorages I was ever purposely in was at a godforsaken place called Macapá, in northeast Brazil. Talk about heat and humidity and rain, rain, rain. It's on the north estuary channel of the Amazon River, the water is coffee colored, the skies thick with black clouds and lightning, and the Equator runs right through the length of the roadstead. I was waiting in the 38-foot yawl *Barbara* to chance my arm on getting out to the offing in the South Atlantic Ocean in between tidal bores.

Because the awesome flow of the Amazon River holds back the ocean tide until a few minutes before the actual time of high tide, it causes a "bore," a hill of sea water up to 17 feet high, which rushes swiftly upstream, so that the estuary water-level rises approximately *40 feet in about six minutes*. One minute your boat's way down amid smelly mud and tree roots, and the next she's hanging on to six thick mooring lines, strained almost to snapping point, up among the topmost branches with howler-monkeys screaming in your ears and snakes dropping on your decks. So, in 1971, just for the hell of it, and I suppose hoping to counter the boredom between bores, I got my mate Conrad Jelinek to lower the anchor of *Barbara* right on the Equator itself: Latitude Zero.

With the mighty Amazon River current ripping through that open roadstead you may guess how much *Barbara* swung this way and that. My mate and I, stopwatch at the ready, confirmed that during *Barbara's* stay in Macapá, she crossed the

27

Equator three times a minute, and our anchor stayed dug in there for exactly three days: 12,960 times "across the line."

So I guess that with the other time *Barbara* had navigated over the Equator (a year before, off Somaliland) she must have done it a *recorded* 12,961 times. I never did claim any world record for that, though there's probably one floating around out there.

There are, weather-wise and for other natural reasons, so many dangerous anchorages that it would be futile for me to even start to list them. The art of navigation and especially coastal pilotage has as much to do with anchoring safely as it does with making safe ocean or coastal passages. But one hazard on remote islands often cannot be foreseen: man-made violence. The most dangerous anchorages in this regard that I was at were both in the Red Sea.

The first was the Brothers Island, which had been the site of a then-dowsed lighthouse. In 1970, however, the Suez Canal was closed, as it had been for years, and unknown to me, was occupied by the Egyptian Army. No sooner had Conrad Jelinek dropped *Barbara*'s hook when suddenly, from this "tourist poster" beach, came a volley of automatic rifle fire. As described in my book *The Incredible Voyage*, we lit out of there. I have never seen an anchor weighed as fast as on that occasion.

My second man-dangerous anchorage was in South Yemen, right on its southern tip. This was in 1986. We had rested in the 40-foot catamaran *Outward Leg* quietly all night, after a very rough passage across the Red Sea from the coast of Sudan, and had restored in sleep our strengths to tackle the notorious strait of Bab El Mandeb the next day.

Suddenly, even as our third hand Sven took the anchor onboard and stowed it, and even as my mate Thomas Ettenhuber fixed our breakfasts in the galley, the sound of voices was heard, then the peculiar snapping rattle of Kalashnikov rifles. As you may imagine, we were off out of there like a bat out of hell. The South Yemenis, seemingly all armed, many shooting, in a fishing boat, chased us probably at full power, while once *Outward Leg* was out of the lee of the northern headland she was purely under main sail. So strong was the wind, a gale from the north, that we were making well over fifteen knots and doubled our distance from our pursuers in ten minutes, and left them wallowing in the offshore swell, waving their rifles.

The most forlorn anchorage I was in was not, as one might have expected, somewhere like Deception Island off the Antarctic Peninsula (there I could bathe in a warm spring well right by the shore, even when the ambient temperature was way below zero Fahrenheit); neither was it among the bergs of the Arctic, nor off some malarial tropical swamp, nor some convict prison-islands (they still existed in the '80s). No; the most depressing anchorage for me without any doubt was in 1984 at Thames Haven, about twenty miles east of London, in the Thames estuary.

It is little more than the entrance to a narrow, muddy creek, where, under cloudy gray skies the water (if that stuff can be so called) is pitch-black, the same color as the mud through which it sluggishly moves. On the top of the stream's bank a huge gray power-station with a monstrous scarlet chimney roared away, with all its lights on, day and night, and, worst of all, there was never, never a living soul in sight, day or night.

Somehow, especially at night, Thames Haven reminded me of the soul-freezing emptiness I had witnessed on the sidewalks in American towns and cities, when all the lights are ablaze and the people who are not driving automobiles, or aimlessly wandering around some shopping mall, are at home, staring at screens, and the streets belong to ghosts and criminals.

But back to Thames Haven in November 1984. Peeping over the after-companionway hatch, through the sleet, it was like watching a horror-film of a world without living people, without music, without the signs which children leave behind them when they finish their play, without any warmth or kindness or beauty. What made being there in *Outward Leg* even more miserable for me was that there was no chance of getting ashore, and the lights, the music and gaiety of London were a mere half-hour away, once I might reach a station and board a train.

With my mate Terry Johannsen, I was bound for the Netherlands and winter was setting in. During a month's so-journ in London, onboard my boat, moored in St. Katherine's Dock very near the Tower of London, I'd been so preoccupied in finishing my book *Outward Leg* that I hadn't been able to contact what few remaining friends of mine were still alive in London. In the whole of the big city I'd met only three people, and one of them had been merely a professional onboard for the night, and didn't really count. It was partly my fault; I didn't much want to meet strangers unless it was vital; I never do in Britain. It's always too much of a tiresome exercise by others in placing me in my proper slot (which, as my exile lengthens, becomes more and more improbable). The older I become the less patience I have for playing games about "who belongs where." There are no class, nor any other distinctions between one person and another in a small craft at sea in a raging storm.

I'd departed St. Katherine's Dock on the outgoing tide, and it was too late to return to London. There could be no going back up the River Thames, even on the incoming tide. Now, in steady downpours, as raindrops reflected in their mil-lions the lights of the power-station, *Outward Leg* perforce skulked in the lee of this ugly, stinking mudbank, in the deaf-ening roar of this huge, ugly, fumes-belching building, and waited for the next outgoing tide, before heading out into the ship-crowded and, at that time of year, because of sudden fog, more than ever, dangerous North Sea.

In the cold and rain of an English November evening,

catching glimpses between downpours at those deathly empty expanses of concrete under the dazzling glare of the power-station lights, I had the impression of being in the ante-room of purgatory. If there is a hell for sailors, I thought to my-self, it must be something similar to being at anchor off Thames Haven in November in the rain. But I was even more naïve then; it was probable that I did not recognize in myself the grief of knowing in my heart that I was at anchor off, within sight of, my own country for the very last time, and that I somehow disguised this knowledge, and blamed, in my mind, my own misery on the makers of the monstrous scene all around me. Then I reflected: there was, there had been, no warmth nor soul comfort for me there; and never had been.

I cannot recall ever, before or since, anywhere in the world, more energetically turning out in a cold wind and sleeting rain at four in the chilly morning to joyfully weigh an-chor and get out to sea, as I did that night off Thames Haven.

Next dawn, as *Outward Leg* wallowed offshore, in the murky yellow waters of the southern North Sea, under a bible-black sky, we both rejoiced anew, my mate Terry and I, in our escape, and yet we shared thoughts of those who, duty-bound, must live lives of quiet despair. We reveled in the wild beauty of where we were, free, and the prospects ahead of us—like all sailors worth their salt, we knew exactly where we were bound. Then, as the Dutch coast loomed low and blue on our southeastern yellow horizon, and grew bolder and more golden, I fumbled onto our tape-player: "Good Morning, America, How Are You?" and very soon Terry seemed to for-get all about Thames Haven and dirty-concrete dreariness, and I myself temporarily dismissed from my thoughts insu-lar-parochialism, and "putting people in their right slot", and unuttered envy of anyone with the chance, the ability, or the courage to get himself out of what, for anyone born below the level of a lord, is and always has been, a cold rainy night. In other words: even as yet again fog closed around us, I was again as close to happiness and content as I shall ever reach in this life.

I've been in so many beautiful anchorages, and anchorages with beautiful vistas, that I am hard-put to choose any single one as the most memorable. Most of those I recall right away seem to have had views of snow-covered mountains in the distance. I recall such vistas from anchorages in Iceland, Greenland, Norway, Antarctica, in the leads of Chile, on the coast of Peru, on Lake Titicaca in Bolivia, and in Algeria, Spain and Morocco.

They were, each one of them, unique, and all almost heart-stirringly lovely. But for my esoteric tastes, to enjoy my stays to the full, although I was often alone, there had to be other interests besides scenic views. Human interests were always precious to me, of course, but also things such as ancient historical sites. There were plenty of these in South America, including the almost-incredible remnants of Inca cities high up in the Peruvian and Bolivian Andes; and in Spain and North Africa many vast relics of the Roman Empire and the Islamic conquests. Intellectually, however, I come, if you like, from ancient Greece, and so my abidingly main ancient-historical interest has always been in ancient Greek civilization and culture.

Mainly my favorite anchorages were any of a score or so on the southwest and south coasts of what is today Turkey. For me there could be no more attractive shorelines on which to anchor anywhere. I don't know about nowadays, but in the early '60s we could not step ashore from our dinghies on some south Turkish beaches without having to shift carefully out of our way wine amphoras washed ashore from shipwrecks over 2000 years before. Then we would picnic on top of huge sarcophagi as long, wide, and deep as a decent-sized yacht, carved in the living stone many centuries before Homer was born. To hike a few miles into the cool hinterland, up beyond the groves of spreading cypress trees, with the gleaming snowy peaks of the high Taurus mountain range ahead in the far distance, wild geese crying overhead and our boat safe at anchor below, and to view, for example, a Greek amphitheater, almost in its original state, yet unvisited for many centuries except by shepherds, was remarkable and memorable; nectar of moments in time. To clamber up steep high cliffs and enter, mouths dry, tongues stopped, limbs aching, chests heaving, huge sculptured tomb caverns carved deep right into the sheer faces well over 3000 years ago was an eerie as well as exhausting experience. I remember how we murmured, when we had recovered our breaths, how to link oneself with the past is a deeply spiritual experience; how we realized an intense humility, perhaps bordering on shame, at the comparatively poor achievements of our own culture, and found such joyful pride in the works of past humanity, and how we learned, with something of a shock, just how similar those ancients, on the surface so alien, so strange, and all dead so long, long ago, must have been, at least mentally, to us. How the devil was it all done without steam or electricity, we wondered. I suppose that now some Turkish government agency has taken charge of all those sites we once roamed so freely, and entry fees are charged.

I must have called onboard my boats over the years at hundreds of tropical coral islands. Such archipelagos as the Bermudas or the Maldives, for example, hold little attraction for me as places to visit except in a sailing yacht to rest for a while on an otherwise long, weary ocean crossing.

I never was much impressed by the traditional Western idea of a "tropical island," as they are depicted so frequently on tourist posters, with the standard-type palm trees drooping over the standard-type, deserted sandy beach and a dead calm flat sea. So far as the tourist islands go, those posters remind me of car advertisements which show the product on a road empty of all other traffic. It can't be called dishonest, but it's surely a bit close to what is now termed "being economical with the truth." In reality those "poster-beach" anchorages are mostly of a kind; when you've experienced one, you've more or less experienced them all. They might be all right as vacation spots for jaded escapees from urbandom, freshly landed from a jumbo jet-plane, but for me the more like a poster a place looks, usually, after a couple of weeks, the more boring it is.

In such places, despite, or perhaps because of, the best efforts of the entertainments providers, for anyone over the age of perhaps 40, there's not much to stay for unless you can depend on your own internal resources. On most poster islands there is generally, once you've learned the local taboos, not much to exercise the mind, not much of real intellectual interest, while the vast majority of non-natives who exile themselves on those flat sort of islands appear to be the very people I would sail ten thousand miles off course to avoid. One of the greatest attractions of cruising in the polar regions is that you simply do not encounter those kind of people, or at any rate not so many of them. But perhaps that has changed, too. Another attraction of polar cruising, I used to keep a straight face as I told people who asked me, was that "it saves buying a fridge."

Hilly islands (the word "Phuket" means hill in Malay) are very often a vastly different story from flat coral islands. They often attract strange and odd characters, and offbeat writers, too. Which is why, to quote a few instances, R.L. Stevenson went to live in Tahiti, Jack London in Hawaii, Ernest Hemingway in Cuba, and Robert Graves in Majorca, and why the hilly islands in the Andaman Sea, or the Azores, or the Canaries, the Antilles, the Comoros, Tahiti, Fiji, or Madagascar all have tales of their own, some of which I'll tell you one day.

Berths Alongside

When I try to look back on all the berths where I've tied up yachts, in my mind I see a dizzying, shifting kaleidoscope of images. Roughly totted up, I must have berthed at well over 3,000 different places in about 100 countries. By berths, I mean places where my boat was tied alongside a jetty or some other kind of structure, or a riverbank, so that I and my crew (if I had one), if we wanted to, could walk directly ashore.

In the New World (in which I include Australia and New Zealand), as soon as the immigrant, slave, or convict ships arrived, people seemed thankfully to have moved ashore and inland, and with memories of steerage misery in mind, just kept going into the vast (to them), almost empty lands. I reckon that's why the majority of North Americans, for example, are not exactly thrilled by ocean yacht racing. They are much more interested in the sky and flying. The forebears of most were, to put it simply, turned off the sea and everything to do with it. In most North American cities, the port is quite separate, and sometimes far away from, the city center. Itinerant labor, the railroad, and finally the automobile made sure the ports stayed well away from town, too.

For most cruisers, sailing in North America is either too inconvenient or expensive. Being anywhere in North America without a car, except for a few cities like New York, Boston, and Seattle, is almost unthinkable. Apart from anything else, the usual attitude towards pedestrians is as it might be, in older cultures, towards suspected criminals. Otherwise, for

35

most, apart from a very few old ports, such as Boston or Annapolis, or South Street Seaport in New York City, to cruise from one city marina to another is perhaps too dull.

In the Old World (in which I include Europe, North Africa, much of Asia and Japan), the cities and towns, before the days of steam or other power afloat and ashore, sent their sailing fleets out from their very hearts. Most ancient port cities or towns have their own haven at, or very close to, their centers. That's why they are so much more picturesque and even beautiful than most of their New World counterparts; the things of sail could not, cannot—help but be beautiful.

I guess my favorite berth of all, when I sort out all the different angles as to why, was in Venice, Italy, in 1970. It was up a side canal of the Grand Canal, and my 40-foot yawl *Barbara* was right alongside a restaurant. It wasn't, so far as I know, a famous restaurant; it seemed to be known only to people living locally. I don't mean our berth was across the street, or fifty yards from the restaurant door; it was right alongside it, across a narrow pavement. Just as in a city you would park a car, so we "parked" *Barbara*, and from our deck into the dining room was just two steps. Not that I needed to go into the dining room. Three friendly and extraordinarily handsome young waiters were only too eager to pass over trays of delicious pasta—cooked by an expert chef—and a bottle of Chianti wine or a cup of steaming espresso coffee whenever my mate Conrad Jelinek and I needed it. You could say it was probably the most culinary-delightful as well as the most quiet and convenient city-berth in the world, besides being picturesque and for me crammed full of interest.

Our views ahead and astern were along an ancient waterway with shaded palaces and cool gardens on either side: the Grand Canal at one end, and a medieval fortress at the other. It was like viewing painted canvases. To see the sun rise over the fort, or go down through a light mist to rest over the

Grand Canal, was like being in a Turner painting, except that the colors, shadows and forms were ever-changing.

Gondolas quietly glided by. The gondoliers wore tight white pants, blue striped shirts, and red bandannas around their heads, and were barefoot. My sailor's eyes noted that the gondolas themselves, unlike the gondoliers, were not shaped symmetrically; as in all worthwhile love affairs, one side was straighter than the other. This was so that the gondolier could keep his paddle on one side of the stern and not have to shift it across the boat, dripping water, over the passengers. The odd shape of the boat would keep it steering straight ahead. I noticed that gondola passengers always spoke in hushed tones. The men passengers seemed subdued, as if by the quick darting glares of their helmsman, while the women basked in radar beams of lust that leapt at them from the same eyes. It was easy, then, to forget that the twentieth century existed.

Earlier, on Venice's Grand Canal itself, we had tied *Barbara* up to one of the red-and-white-striped gondola mooring posts right by the main entrance to the Gritti Palace Hotel, one of the world's finest, for someone who had been with us to go ashore. From our berth at the hotel, we had been only a couple of hundred yards away from the Doge's Palace, the Bridge of Sighs and St. Mark's Square. We could not stay there, but that was no hardship, for the continual noise of powerboat and ferry engines would have driven us away in any case.

All things considered, the old city of Venice, with its complete lack of automobiles, buses, and trucks; its quaint streets and intelligent, civilized, pleasant, good looking inhabitants; and above all its convenient and interesting berths, is the world's finest city to visit afloat in a yacht.

Another beautiful city to visit in a yacht is unfortunately not on the itinerary of most ocean yachts. This is the city (or rather two cities) of Budapest, over 800 miles up the River Danube. There, in 1985, in the San Diego-registered trimaran *Outward Leg*, we berthed alongside a pontoon floating in the

Danube directly off Roosevelt Square. The river there is about
150 yards wide and flows around beautiful islands, which are
city parks. Even in communist days, the Hungarian Parlia-
ment and other old Hapsburg buildings were well-
maintained and extremely impressive.

Surprisingly, on reflection, farther upstream in Vienna,
our berth had not been as pleasant as the one in Budapest was
to be. The Vienna-Danube Canal is a stone-faced ditch running close to the Vienna city center. It reminded me of an over-
grown janitor. It is big, but not impressive; all the surrounding
buildings turn their backs on it, as if in disdain. There is no
traffic for good reason: the current through it is between eight
and ten knots. Enter it only if you would die to sleep close to
the Opera House and the Vienna Boys Choir. Otherwise, stay
on the banks of the River Danube itself. You will be surrounded by dusty or oily quays, noisy barges and tugs, and
the rusty ruin of Adolph Hitler's old trans-Danube road-
bridge, but at least you'll stand a good chance of leaving your
berth without the current gripping your keel and smashing
your boat into something very solid, like granite.

In northern Europe, one of the best berths was alongside
the canal wall of the Maritime Museum in Amsterdam,
Netherlands. Going ashore on foot (on one foot, for me), was
not very convenient, but once in our dinghy, we could flash
through the city canals much faster than any car, and shop just
about anywhere. In Amsterdam, I doubt if anything important to civilized life is more than a few steps from one canal or
another. Grocery store, greengrocer, fruit shop, chemist, hospital, clinic, post office, railroad station, police station, brothel,
bar, cafe, restaurant, you name it; there was navigable water
flowing past its front door.

For us as yachties, the greatest thing about the Netherlands was that there was never anyone waiting on the jetty to
tell us gleefully what we could *not* do, or how much we had
to pay, as there would invariably be in Britain, and especially

southern England. There half the population seemed to be made up of port officials, uniformed or not, waiting with a fine or a fee-charge ready to thrust at us as soon as we tied up. At the same time, they usually had muttered a list of forbidden activities. In nine cases out of ten, the longer the muttered list, the earlier the town went dead. In 1984, I was unpleasantly surprised at this. Twenty-two years before, on my previous visit, there had been little interference by busybodies. Now they were everywhere, It must have been the sight of *Outward Leg*'s Old Glory American ensign that dragged them, pencils, charge-sheets, and bills in hand, from their sausage-and-chips, tellies, and pints of warm beer.

In the '50s and '60s, there were few yacht marinas anywhere outside of North America, Mainly, when cruising, we called at fishing ports. While noisy, smelly, and often dirty, they were cheap to moor in and frequently great fun. One of my favorites was Marsala, on the southwestern tip of Sicily. There were so many fishing boats working out of there that once a yacht (in the normal "musical chairs" in working ports) was nudged and shoved all the way to the town-end of the fishing port, it was a very slow job getting out again. The fact that Marsala is a wine-growing area, and the juice flowed thick and cheap, did not make the job of getting back out to sea any quicker either, as you may guess.

The island of Malta, too, was cheap. There were about a thousand empty yacht berths, all right next to neighborhood streets. The capital, Valetta, was impressive, with all the fortifications around its harbor. But it had been a British possession, so the tax man's presence always threatened, and real joy was almost absent, so we avoided it if we could. The same with Cyprus. Alexandria, Egypt, with all its fun, was too near.

Before Morocco took it over, Tangier catered for every sin. Its small port was at the bottom of a steep hill which led up to the casbah, the Arab quarter. In the mid-50s, it was the hangout of thieves, con men, smugglers, and other rogues. It was in Tangier's casbah, in a French-run brothel, at the age of thirty-two, while drinking beer (brothels were the only places one could drink without being pestered by scrofulous beggars), that I had first become conscious of actually *listening* to a piece of music. It had been Ravel's *Bolero*. The occasion awoke in me an interest in, and a need to hear, European classical music that have never diminished. In fact, as I grow older, they become more acute. In all my boats after 1956, I had a hand wind-up phonograph and played on it, over and over, any classical records I could afford: Beethoven, Brahms, Mozart, Bach, Handel, Tchaikovsky, Mendelssohn. If those composers had not lived and written down their scores, and if those records had not been made, my life since my early thirties would have been hardly worth living most of the time, but especially when I was alone.

One of the most beautiful berths I ever tied up at was also one of the strangest for an ocean-yacht: in Bolivia, at the tiny port of the island of Taquila, on Lake Titicaca. The harbor itself, protected by rock walls, was no bigger than the average suburban front yard. The port entrance was so narrow that my cutter *Sea Dart*, which was a mere seven feet wide, only just managed to scrape through the entrance. What a breathtaking place it was. It was the stuff of dreams, of fantasy. It was cozy and at the bottom of 800 ancient steep steps leading to a Quechua-Indian village. The view from the harbor was of a wide sweep of blue mountains to the west. But to climb the step up the hill, up another 1000 feet . . . from there, along the horizons, across the wide lake, to the north, the east, and the south, the views were stunning: 350 miles of the Andes Mountains, snow-covered and gleaming, silver in the mornings, scarlet and gold in the dusks, rising another 7000 feet higher than the 13,500 feet I was already at. That view was truly *El Dorado*.

Back in New York City, in 1976, when I was writing my book *The Incredible Voyage*, for relief and what might pass for fresh air I used to step outside my cramped apartment on

West 10th Street and amble down to the West Side Highway. I would gaze at the Statue of Liberty in the far distance, across the Hudson River, and then south at the skyscrapers of the World Trade Center. Then daydreaming silently, for I could never bring myself to tell anyone else in case they thought me crazy, I would reflect that I had sailed an ocean-vessel much, much higher than the tops of those buildings, much higher than anyone had dreamed of before. With little *Sea Dart*, through gales and storms for thousands of miles, and man-made as well as natural perils, I had reached the highest navigation ever to be made until man finds water among the stars.

In 1977, I found myself and *Sea Dart* in the most surrealistic yacht berth anyone can ever imagine. This was on the stage of the Cavendish ballroom, seven floors above street level, in the Waldorf-Astoria on Park Avenue in Manhattan. We were guests of the Explorers Club, along with an astronaut and other explorers.

It was at that same Explorers Club dinner in 1977 that, in response to an English fellow-explorer's reference to the "discovery by Columbus of America," I observed that all Columbus had actually found was that America had already been discovered. At the time, my comment before that august audience raised nothing but silence and a few eyebrows. Now, in 1994, the President of the Explorers Club, in introducing himself, is anxious that everyone should be aware of his own "Native American" antecedents. So much for the advance of "political correctness."

EPISODE 6

High and Dry

Next day, the fifteenth of April, with Don being driven in his car to shoot pictures, the truck trundled through the garbage-strewn grime and over the potholes of upper Manhattan. By 3:00 P.M. the hauler had skillfully maneuvered his leviathan close into the loading bay of the Waldorf Astoria. By 4:00 P.M. a heavy fork-lift had unloaded *Sea Dart* and her trolley, all three tons of them, off the truck and onto the sidewalk, with Don taking pictures and helping where he could. Soon the hauler ground off, his job (and a fine job, too) done. The fork-lift disappeared as magically as it had arrived. Don and I were left with the boat.

"What do we do now, Tristan?" asked Don.

"Shove her inside the elevator," I replied, putting my weight onto her stern. "I've got exactly three hours to get her onto the stage in the ballroom," I told him to the fascination of a dozen passers-by who had stopped in their tracks at the sight—unusual even for Manhattan.

"You're going to need some help," Don observed.

"Let's get her in the elevator first. Don, give us a hand here," I puffed. Don looked at me nonplussed for a moment.

"The old *fait accompli*," I explained.

"The what?" Don grinned. He was getting to know me by now.

"Latin for 'here it is, mate—and here it stays.'" I heaved my heavy lever again.

It took Don and me about half an hour to lever the trolley

into the elevator foyer. I was concentrating all my energy now, mental as well as physical, into inching *Sea Dart* closer to her goal. Someone tapped me on the shoulder. A voice demanded, "What the hell *is* this?" Without looking to face my inquisitor I grunted, "It's a boat . . . going . . . to . . . the ballroom."

"A what . . . goin' where? . . . I'm hotel security."

I let go of the great wooden lever. I turned to face him, breathing hard.

He was a tall, hefty man of about my age, silver haired, wearing spectacles and a gray business suit. "I'm hotel security," he repeated. He showed me a badge of some kind.

"An' that thing isn't going inside this hotel."

"But she's due for the Explorers Club dinner!" I expostulated.

"That's neither here nor there," said the security officer. "It isn't going in—for one thing . . . " He stood back to inspect her. " . . . it's too damned big to get into the elevator, an' for another it's going to create a hazard, an' for another if you get it inside it's going to cause a lotta damage . . . "

I was getting riled now. "Do you know the chief maintenance engineer?" I asked him.

"Why, sure . . . but . . . "

"Can you contact him, please?"

"What for? He can't spare any staff to help . . . "

"I don't want any help . . . "

"Whaddaya want?"

"I want two electric saws . . . "

"Saws?"

"Yes . . . because this boat's come four thousand miles to attend this function and she's going in, even if I have to cut her up into little pieces and stick her together again inside!"

The security officer studied me. I stood with one foot in front of me and one hand on *Sea Dart*'s gunwale. He was silent for a moment, then he said quietly, "Hey, you're some guy, ya know that? Wait here a minute . . . " He disappeared into the receiving office and picked up a phone.

While the security man was away, Russell Gurney showed up. In a second he had his coat off (America!America!) and he, too, was heaving at another lever. Now there were three of us shoving the boat. In minutes the security man, with two hotel-staff, all in their shirt sleeves, without saying a word, were grunting and pushing along with us.

Govannon entered me. I grabbed the guardrail stanchions, one inch-thick rods of cast steel that made her too high to enter, and bent them over like putty with my bare hands. I severely strained my stomach muscles doing it, but I consoled myself that what will bend can always be straightened again. (The rails took a week—my stomach two years.)

How we—by now eight of us (the reception office staff had been drawn into *Sea Dart's* magic vortex)—got her into the elevator was a miracle. When the job was finished, she was positioned diagonally athwart the machine's floor. Fore and aft, when the doors shut there was no more than a sixteenth of an inch to spare. Between the top of her doghouse and the heavy wire-netting roof of the elevator, you could not have inserted a cigarette paper sideways.

As we got her ready to slide into the elevator, the hotel staff stared.

The fit in the elevator was so tight that only one person could go up the four stories with the boat.

"Skipper's job," Russell puffed.

"The very man himself," I said as I wedged myself horizontally onto her foredeck in the dark with an eighth of an inch to spare.

When the elevator stopped and the gates opened, I struggled down from my perch and stretched myself. Then I walked around a tight corner and went to reconnoiter the track through the great kitchens. I was as quick as I could, but not quick enough. When I returned from checking that the way was clear through the Cavendish Room, into the kitchen, the sight that met my eyes was *remarkable*.

All around were steaming vats and stainless steel ovens. The air was warm, but not oppressively so. Through it wafted a dozen delicious cooking aromas. Scullery hands rushed around, there was a noisy clatter of utensils. Chefs and their assistants in their varieties of curious tall white headgear were stirring their concoctions and mixing their magic, now and then gazing, astonished, at the sight of a seagoing sailing boat moving slowly but surely right through their kitchen with only a fraction of an inch to spare on either side of her. It was *surrealistic.* I hesitated for a moment, taking in the sight, fixing it in my memory. *Sea Dart* was enjoying all this attention and cosseting. She was like a crotchety old queen being wheeled through the castle kitchen to check on the expenditures. I grinned at her, then grabbed the rope on the forward end of her trolley and heaved with all my might.

She passed through the doorways from the kitchens into the inner corridors with hardly a paint-coat's thickness to spare each side of her after we had removed the doors from their hinges. Above her, the space between her doghouse roof and the door lintels was less than a thirty-second of an inch. When her full height was passing through you could not see daylight between her and the door cross-beam. Tavan and Govannon were still with us. Dagda's caldron was just ahead. It was as if someone were pushing the doorposts apart and lifting the lintels to let her pass.

Heaving, shoving, and pushing, by now there were a dozen Americans all puffing, blowing and shouting to each other in English, Spanish, and French (four sous-chefs, going off duty, had fallen under *Sea Dart*'s spell), all helping her to her destination.

By six o'clock she was in the Cavendish Room. Here, again the scene was out of this world. The room was a spacious chamber, half as big as a football field, all carpeted and hung with tapestries. Around the walls sat silver-painted furniture upholstered in red. In the center of the molded ceiling hung a chandelier with more than a hundred lights—and under the chandelier a dozen men danced attendance on an unbelievably battered nineteen-foot ocean sailing boat's hull. She *loved* it.

Russell measured the last remaining doorways between the boat and the ballroom. There had been an afternoon function. We had not been able to get to them since the operation commenced. Soon he was back with a serious face. Behind us, as *Sea Dart* had passed, the way back was now closed off, with all the doors replaced and the kitchens going at full blast for dinner. Russell used a phrase that I thought was colorful. "We've painted her into a corner, Tristan," he said. "She's too high to go through into the ballroom. We'll never take her off the trolley."

"Too high?"

"Yes, by two inches." It was now six-thirty. We had half an hour to spare. "And it looks like we're not going to be able to manage it. There's no way we can lift her without a big car jack—and that's going to put too much strain on the floor in one place . . . It looks like she'll have to stay out here . . . " His face was glum. "I guess the guests will just have to be content seeing her out here, outside the ballroom . . . " All around us sweaty faces saddened. There was silence except for an almost apologetic shuffle of embarrassed feet.

Seafarers see things differently from landsmen. A vessel is not a thing . . . she is the sum total of all her voyages, past, present, and future, and every emotion that ever goes into her . . . love, strength, care . . . *determination* . . .

I looked at the security officer. His shoulders dropped a little. I turned to Don—he was studying me, waiting. I looked at the others who had spent their free time helping *Sea Dart*. It was as if they were all trying to read my thoughts.

"She promised to get to the stage, Russ," I said finally. "Can you get me a saw?"

"What . . . you're not going to cut her up?" Russell exploded.

"Don't say anything, please . . . Just get me a saw."

While Russ was gone to his car there was a wondering silence among the crew. Then one French-American sous-chef, still in his white kitchen gear, climbed down from the cockpit, where he had been inspecting the cabin, peering inside, murmuring "Wonderfool—wonderfool, ze workmansheep!"

"Treestan," he said. He was very young, perhaps twenty or so. "You cannot cut up all zat beautifool wood in zere . . . ze workmansheep . . . " He was almost crying. " 'Ow can you own a boat like zees and cut into 'er?"

"I know," I said, "it's like cutting into my own heart—but her destination is just as much a part of her as her doghouse. Her destination cannot be repeated or replaced—her doghouse can."

The logic appealed to the Frenchman in him. But he still stood back and shook his head and murmured, *Putain! Fous le camp!*

At a quarter to seven, the doghouse was sawed away from the deck. At seven *Sea Dart* was on the five-foot-high stage behind the curtains. By seven-thirty I had her sails hauled up, by seven-forty I had showered and changed into the requisite tuxedo, and by eight o'clock the function commenced.

Previously published in *Adrift* (1980; 1992)

My Favorite City

Younger people than I (that now means most people) often ask me: "What was the best place you ever visited?" My stock response is, "It depends on what you mean by best, on what your interests are . . . "

Other seafarers are usually interested in what were the sailing conditions and the attitudes of locals (for most males read *women* and curiously enough, for most women read *women*) ashore, and the availability of yacht gear and repairs. If it is tourists who ask, naturally what intrigues them are travel, hotels, restaurants, food, and night life, but *costs* always interest everyone.

Over half a century and more, I've sailed around islands and coastal villages the world over, most of which were cheap places, but, while fine for sea, sand, and sunshine, they were otherwise for me in some ways rather dull. While I doubt I could be called a highbrow, my own interests include (among other, perhaps even more important, more sybaritic needs) classical music, architecture, and art. All, usually, mean *cities*.

The five most value-for-money and exciting cities I was ever in were: *Tangier* in the late '40s and early '50s; *Beirut* in the mid '50s to mid '60s (there was *nothing* unavailable in both. I can't comment on the quality of what was on offer; in my 30s and 40s I was far too young to be much discerning); *Barcelona* in the late '50s (but a poverty-stricken, sad city, under an appalling dictatorship); *Constanta*, Romania, in '85 and '90 (but with a fistful of *lei* notes there was nothing to buy). But the one city that always comes back fondly to my mind, again and again, although it had no beach, as by far the most exciting, most cultured, most beautiful, most elegant and yet the cheapest of them all was *Buenos Aires*, Argentina, in the mid-70s.

In early '75, my little cutter *Sea Dart* was berthed at Olivos, about 15 miles west of Buenos Aires city-center. Foreign yachts were rare (and still are, but to a lesser degree). I had a free berth in a lovely old-fashioned yacht-haven, as guest of the Yacht Club Argentino, which also lent me an apartment. One of my neighbors was the aging Martin Bormann, Hitler's heir, who had escaped from Germany in 1945, and since hidden in South America.

In those days Argentina had steep inflation; modern bank communications had not reached Buenos Aires. Anyway, the street exchange rate for the pound sterling was often an enormous number of times the official rate at the bank. For one pound I often received in pesos the bank-equivalent of as many as 200 pounds. The strange thing was that there were then as yet no outer signs of this inflation. No one seemed to be suffering any more than would be normal in the mid '70s in any other Western city the size of Buenos Aires (which is more European than Paris). Most people were well-dressed; there were no beggars, and I never saw a hungry looking person in Buenos Aires. There were, even, very few street hawkers.

I would rise in my apartment in Olivos about 11 A.M. after the previous night's exertions, have a good breakfast of steak, egg and chips for a few pennies. Then I would travel by modern, well-kept, fast train to Buenos Aires main station. A weekly return ticket cost four cents. There, in the crowded Edwardian station-concourse, by a statue to Eva Perón, always piled high with magnificent wreaths of flowers as tributes from the poor, would be several money-changers. We would make a deal surreptitiously; Isabel Perón's goons were everywhere. I would hand the man an English pound; he would hand me a thick roll of peso notes.

I would step outside the station, pass by a miniature Big Ben clocktower and walk by the city park, at the main gate of which stood a huge notice in Spanish forbidding entrance to anyone not wearing a jacket and tie. This despite the 95 degree Fahrenheit midday heat.

On one typical visit to the city center, I bought a pair of brand-new genuine cowhide leather shoes, and two cotton shirts. I ate a well-served, delicious steak lunch in an elegant restaurant. In Buenos Aires, steaks were huge; they drooped over the edges of dinner plates. After lunch, I visited a couple of bars. My acquaintances, being poor, enjoyed my largesse for a pair of hours. Then one close friend and I attended a concert by the Buenos Aires Philharmonic. Emerging at 11 P.M. we took a taxi out to a suburb and, while our taxi awaited us for two hours, its driver eating his steak supper on me, we enjoyed a huge meal to the strains of a tango band, and watched Portenos (Buenos Aires locals) disport to that intricate and graceful dance. We returned to the city center, paid off our taxi, and visited several *el ambiente* bars.

My young friend had been forcibly exiled from Chile by the military government of General Augusto Pinochet, and needed to be at the Buenos Aires Police Department early next day, so there was no question of our repairing to my apartment at Olivos. Instead I booked both of us into a small hotel, a double room with a balcony overlooking the city, air-conditioning and a bathroom, and I stayed there until noon next day.

My second day in Buenos Aires was more or less the same as the first, except that I bought only socks; my partner and I took the midnight train to Olivos to stay the night in my apartment.

The morning after that particular run, back at Olivos, when I reckoned up the cost of my whole past thirty-six hours, a pair of new shoes, two shirts, a pair of socks, innumerable beers for myself and many others, taxi fares, two classical concerts, a cinema show, a night for two in a hotel, and twelve meals (half of them steaks) with at least one bottle of wine on each occasion, the whole amount I'd spent was the equivalent of just *one U.S. dollar and twenty cents*. I'd had to re-calculate over and over again, but it was true.

In Buenos Aires in early '75 there seemed to be few foreigners besides myself. I can hardly recall meeting any, except a couple of American merchant-seamen. But such travelers' dream-times are always short. This one lasted from January to the end of April 1975. Then it was time for me to get out; the political scene was ever more violent, and daily there were more and more "disappeared."

But for me from a cost viewpoint it sure was great while it lasted. Just imagine: pigging it like that for four whole months for a mite less than *one hundred and fifty dollars*. Of course my boat suffered; I was too busy having fun to maintain her properly. Nothing comes free.

I'd seen both the Peróns close-up in Buenos Aires back in '49. I'd been in a British warship which called there. It had been at a military parade. Evita had been splayed, arms and legs outstretched, laughing, clad in a diaphanous, sparkling ballroom gown, over the front of an army tank as it roared at the head of a long armored column through the city. Staring down from a Victorian-style balcony had been her husband Juan Perón. To me he looked more like a sugar daddy softie than a General or Dictator. Evita was one *hard lady*. Madonna is all about *show*; Evita was all about *power*: pure, undisguised, ultimately asexual, and utterly vulgar, and *she knew it*. That's why we laughed *with her and not at her*.

EPISODE 8

Scares

I've lost count of the number of times that people have asked me what were the most frightening experiences I've had in fifty years of seafaring. I usually answer the question with a joke—something like: "Oh, one time when I was chartering in the Greek Islands; I had some passengers joining and one of them was listed as Mrs. Thatcher;" you know the kind of thing . . . Here I won't count my five years Navy war-time, even though they were spent mostly on North Atlantic convoys in fairly small craft like destroyers and frigates. Much of that was bloody frightening indeed, although I suppose there's some comfort in having company on such occasions, and in knowing that anyway someone else is in charge. Neither do I count the capsizing iceberg in the Arctic: that was so unique and terrifying an occasion as to be beyond most ordinary mortals' comprehension, thank God. Another time I don't count was when my 24-foot Folkboat was smashed to bits in mid-Atlantic, simply because there was no time to be frightened: the whole episode was over in less than a minute. That was in 1968. It is only in hindsight that it is terrifying. Occasionally, even now, I have a nightmare of it.

In my 37 years of voyaging under sail, the two times which I do count, though, occurred both when I was single-handing. They always strike my mind and emotions when this question is asked, but I've never told anyone much about them. Both times other marine animals besides me were involved. The way I tell these tales might offend some conservationists, but believe me, the bottom line when you are alone on the ocean is to conserve yourself, because if you don't you'll be dead.

The first time was in the northern autumn of 1968; a portent perhaps of the whale encounter which I mentioned before and which happened a couple of weeks later. I'd departed from Vigo, in northwest Spain, in my 24-foot engine-less Folkboat *Two Brothers*, headed for the Azores and eventually, I had hoped, for South America and Lake Titicaca. The wind in these parts is usually a north-westerly, but a few hours after I slipped port it veered and blew quite strongly from the southwest. This forced me northward into the Bay of Biscay. As usual when any kind of blow strikes up, the bay became rough; the best thing to do is get out of it into the open ocean; I hauled around for the northwest, to escape into the deeper, more steady North Atlantic. As suddenly as the wind had risen, it dropped again and left me wallowing away with the mainsail slatting this way and that for thirty hours, until there was a dead flat calm.

Over the slowly-moving, undulating sea-hills, I could still see the mountains of Galicia, mist-shrouded at their peaks, 25 miles to the south. So there I was, becalmed. It was fairly cold; I was wearing two jerseys and two pairs of corduroy pants. In those days, you couldn't beat corduroys for cold-weather sailing; not like now with all these fancy pants developed for skiers and such. Cords were cheap, too.

I remember I'd just finished my lunch. As I washed my plate over the side, I realized that the sea, instead of being its usual greeny-blue, was almost black. I stared at this for a second, until I realized that *Two Brothers* was surrounded five to ten feet underwater by whales. Not a mere one or two; not a dozen, but a factual, living, breathing, moving, racing, menacing one hundred—at least —of the buggers. Many of them must have been shifting at twenty knots. One surfaced, and I saw that it was a narwhal. That one must have been all of

twenty feet long and he must have weighed a good ten tons.
They were probably feeding off small fish; pilchards most
likely. I was too frightened, with all those moving masses
threatening to collide with my boat, to think about their feeding habits. I stared straight down into the water; three narwhals were basking in the shade of my boat, lying
athwartships no more than a foot below my keel. Now and
again one would rub its fin—I could feel the boat shudder
every time. Within half a minute, even under two jerseys and
a jacket, I was perspiring freely. I tried to recall the prayers I
had learned as a child in Wales. That was the day my beard
turned gray.

That herd of narwhals stayed with *Two Brothers* for three
and a half hours, and I've never, not even in steamer-crowded
fog nor in any storm, felt the same doom-laden terror. Then,
as suddenly as the great cumbersome animals had appeared,
they all left. Once again I was left in the safety of ocean-borne
solitude. That evening the wind rose from the northwest, and
I was again underway and happy.

The second time I was really terrified was in 1972 off the
coast of Peru, in my 18-foot waterline cutter *Sea Dart*. We all
know that the Humboldt Current, as it runs north from the
Antarctic, carries along with it some pretty strange creatures.
It's a foggy area, because of the hot sun and cold sea-water.
Again, even though I was just south of the Equator, I was
wearing two jerseys. I'd been at sea, heading south for Callao,
beating against the prevailing southerly breeze and the
bloody old Humboldt Current, for about sixty days and
nights. I know I was not hallucinating—I'll tell you later about
a couple of times that I did—and neither was I drunk; there
had been no booze within miles of me for months. Beating out
into the ocean, but not so much as to get carried too offshore
in the day, and beating inshore, but not so much as to run
ashore, at night, is the name of the game on the West Coast of
South America, heading south. But sometimes, inshore, the

wind would die; I would be carried back north by the merciless Humboldt. Near the land the seas were calm, when that happened. The fog at sea-level is burned off by the sun about noon; then the heat is enough to fry what brains we have, but the revealed scenery, the snow-capped Andes! I couldn't sit staring at the snowy peaks all day; I turned to gaze over the side.

What met my eyes was enough to make a bishop burn his Bible. All around and under—just under, one or two feet under—the boat, was a blood-red gooey mass. It was round, undulating, so that it appeared to my horror-stricken eyes as if it were breathing, and it extended out about twenty feet from the boat. All around the periphery of this monstrous scarlet mass there were tentacles waving out another ten feet or so. Some of them curled up and reached menacingly above the surface of the seas; some of them only inches away from my gunwales.

Even as I gaped further I saw that riding on the seas all around, just below the surface, were other monstrous beings, giant jellyfish or whatever they were, and some were blue, some green, some inky black. When I came to my senses I dragged out of its carton my never-yet-used four-horsepower British Seagull outboard motor, fumbled it onto its stern mounting, scrambled around panic-struck for gasoline, prayed like a maniac and pulled the ripcord. It started the first time and I got out of that patch of horrible color as fast as I could, all the while hoping to hell that the engine noise and the prop wash would not enrage those things—whatever they were.

I told this tale a few times afterwards; for some years it was scoffed at. Recently, however, there have been reportings by scientists of these giant "jellyfish" in the Humboldt Current—so it must be true. There are more things on Earth than are dreamed of, but I'm convinced there are many, many more in the sea.

Departures

These days, I suppose not many yacht skippers use the word "departure." More than likely they use terms such as "push off" or "shove off" or simply "leave." "Leave" will not do. How can anyone "leave" and begin at the same time? But a departure is both.

"To make a departure" expresses something stately. It gives a sense of occasion. But regardless of how stately the word or the act, all vessels, of whatever size, share in the symbolic significance of departure: is it a leaving or a beginning? Every time I have made a departure, I have been torn between what remained undone ashore and the joy of release from everything past. At the bittersweet moment of casting off, there was usually the ghost of anxiety or doubt—to cross an ocean is not a small endeavor. I would then exorcize it by shouting "Let the party start!"

On occasions, in Scotland, before setting off on a long voyage, I would, with a small knapsack on my back, walk up a winding narrow harbor road and turn off at a windswept rock towards a distant peak. Sometimes I would cadge a car-ride, or even pay a bus ticket, up into the mountains. Once the vehicle had trundled off and I was left alone, I would sit, or walk slowly. I simply devoured with my eyes rocks and mountain peaks and green grass and tried to surfeit myself with the mountain masses of Caledonia that lay before me. Now that the prospect of the voyage lay immediately before my mind, I had the urge to savor the firmness of dry land, for once I sailed I would be seeing nothing but the sea for a month or more. Then I would try to convince myself that I was thoroughly tired of stone and solid earth and wanted nothing more than to get down to sea level, sail out, and get to know the sea again. But even now, with dozens of long voyages, and a thousand little ones, notched on my knife-sheath, I still feel a memorial chill on casting off, as the gulls jeer and the empty mainsail claps.

Characteristically, in those days, before I made my departures, I did not bother to obtain clearance papers, registration, bill of health, or even evidence of ownership. Most officials at my destinations, especially in Latin America, were always too astonished, not to say impressed, to bother with such mundane matters. As for the official who was not impressed, or who stuck to the book, there was always a powerful local yacht-club member who could threaten to stop his pension, or have him transferred to a jungle-border hut, if he carried on at me for lack of bits of paper. They were far simpler days for ocean yachtsmen.

In northern Europe, you never could tell how a departure would be, weather-wise, and you learned to take every inch the Gods allowed. Many times I would be all ready to depart, then stick my head out of the companionway hatch and find that I could not; there was a thick white mist over everything, so that I could not see the bowsprit of my own boat. Everything would be damp; the very deck smelled of fog . . .

Most of my departures, all over the globe, were quiet. There was one memorable occasion though, a long time ago and far, far away, when a lover came to the jetty even as I was casting off, and in a time-honored fashion, leaned over and tied a long green ribbon to my mainstay. I never forgot that. I've had many lovers, but the Green Ribbon stands out first in my memories. It's an age-old custom (from the Celtic ages) that seems to have died out. I saw it regularly as a child, but cannot recall witnessing it less than thirty-five years ago. It should be revived. That green ribbon can, with the right strength winds, last the whole voyage long, and serve as a reminder that all love, for a sailor, is not merely for and in and of the sea alone.

One autumn departure, from Dartmouth, England, back in the mid-'50s, in the 46-foot yawl *Virginia W*, was very quiet indeed. No lovers there; only harbormasters' bills unpaid. Dazed with activity, I scarcely noticed when *Virginia W* moved out into the tidal stream, away from the mud and the jetty which she might have been considering, so many weeks had we been there, her final resting place. Officialdom was much slacker in those days; I doubt if anyone noticed that I'd departed until next day, and probably not then if it had been raining hard. There was no chance for nostalgic farewells to England, no melancholy or happy leaning on guard-rails, no waving to friends. Instead of dropping gentle tears, I sweated and hauled on lines and got the anchor onboard at last, and the thing was done. I had chosen my weather, I had chosen my tide; I was off to sea. Once outside the harbor entrance, I quickly took in the ensign (expensive things, red ensigns), hoisted the mizzen, cast off the mainsheet, swayed the halyards, and neatly coiled them, took the wheel and the mainsheet in hand, and off *Virginia W* went, like a cat let off a leash. An hour after dusk, on the ebb tide, I got clear of the approaches to the harbor, and the sails and the tiller to a very light northwesterly. I stood in the companionway, with the warmth from the galley stove against my back and facing the cold fresh breeze, watched the dark water slowly drown the blinking lights astern, and England was gone. The wind moaned aloft, the pipe turnbuckles whistled a high note, the stanchions a low note, and the booms, lifting and falling with each roll of the ship, creaked the sheet blocks as I sang on my way southwest. There was a sleepy murmur of waters cast aside. She was off to sea.

But I remember very well how I felt as I sang to cheer myself. If there is ever a feeling of high endeavor in setting out to challenge and ocean—I was bound direct for Tenerife—, the slightest aura of glory, of courage, of heroism, it certainly did not attend my performance. I was depressed and overawed by the prospect before me. That night was not auspicious for good winds. There was a tired breeze which hardly ruffled the sea. Then, towards dawn, *Virginia W* felt her first ground swells. The land of Cornwall still guarded her, but now, over her bows, lay a line of rolling ocean, shining and cold. Her mainsail and mizzen, with a balloon jibsail, filled with breeze, and tried to drive the bows under, but the forward sections resisted, passing sea harmlessly over her shoulder, sending spray into my tired, but content face. The misty, unclear land fell astern by noon, and by early afternoon our departure from England was completed. I hove to and slept.

Another departure I recall well was from Vigo, in northwest Spain. In the mid-50s, not many yachts were fitted with reliable engines; sometimes we resorted to being towed out to sea by fishing boats or tugs. Sometimes we had to—by official order. In the 38-foot ketch *Angela* I'd been at anchor in the fjord-like harbor for three weeks, waiting for the owner, who lived in New Zealand, to send me some money for stores and repairs. It was in the spring. This day there was, I remember, a cold snap in the air. I singled up our mooring, that is, passed one line through the ring on the buoy and back on board, so I could just let go of the line and *Angela* would be free. After a couple of hours, a huge harbor tug approached and passed me a towline that was a good foot around. This I tied to my bow sponson. A few minutes later, with me gesturing to the Spanish tug skipper to slow down—slow down!—we passed the bluffs at the harbor entrance, and almost as soon as her forefoot lifted to the first long Atlantic swell, the tow line was let go. To the cheers and waves of the tug crew (everyone in Vigo knew I was bound for the West Indies—ocean passages were extremely rare in those days), I crowded sail on *Angela* as fast as I could. Up main, up mizzen, up jib, and away.

I never felt anything more delightful than the first rise

and fall of the ship to the scend of the sea. After so many weeks of lifeless equilibrium, the canting decks and long resistless heave and roll of the hull gave me a sense of freedom and exhilaration impossible to describe. As sail after sail was sheeted home and the yacht laid steeply over to the freshening breeze, I would not have changed places with the captain of the Royal Yacht. Each to his taste, and mine to a yawl setting sail. Gaining the open water, *Angela* felt the bracing breeze wax fresh. She tossed the quick foam from her bows, as a young colt tosses his snortings.

Tropical departures I remember by the score. I often had a crew in the tropics—heat makes for harder effort, and also in many areas a foreign yacht needs a guard when the skipper is ashore. In the early dawn at Ko Phi Phi in the Andaman Sea we rattled the anchor chain in and got the hook onboard. Just after 5 A.M. *Gabriel*'s headsail filled and she swung away from the sleeping cove. In the short dawn of the tropics, I could already see the small headland gliding towards me, that tiny cape that marked the division between the two worlds of enclosed waters and open sea: it sloped gently down to the water verdant and tautly arched, like a dancer's pointed foot in a green ballet-shoe. Then we rounded the headland and were underway along the steep bluffs, with a cooler, damp land breeze laden with mysterious, sensuous perfumes of exotic flowers. We moved silently, without a wave upon the purple water, and gauged our progress by the movement of Sirius, the brightest star, along the hilltops. Soon, faint and changing colors traced patterns in the east, creeping slowly through the sky like frost on windowpanes. Then suddenly and wondrously the golden sun leaped into sight and day once more was ours.

In the days before weather satellites, forecasting of hurricanes was much less accurate; in the Atlantic to be on the safe side I aimed for Trinidad, south of the usual hurricane tracks. "Trinidad for Christmas and mail from home!" was the thought that, I imagined, would bring my anchor on deck in Tenerife.

But just before departure, the French owner had showed up in an escort boat and insisted that I head for Martinique, then a French colony. Otherwise he said, "No Martinique, no pay." We delivery-skippers had no union.

Touche, a 36-foot sloop, had been in France with her owner and crew. I had been in France, too, to meet the owner and pick up the boat. On the ocean crossing, all went well. As usual on French yachts, there was enough food onboard to last for many months.

The day of reckoning arrived. Off Martinique I searched beneath all four bunks for francs and centimes, turned all my own pockets inside out, and soberly counted my wealth: a little less than 100 francs. There would be a week to wait until the owner arrived and took me to a yacht I was to deliver to France.

Was this an arrival or a departure? What is the difference? I spent the time in Martinique wondering this and awaiting *Touche*'s owner, and my payment. With only money for bare shore-side necessities, I sat on the side of the road, studying the locals and planning my next departure, to deliver a 40-foot ketch the same Frenchman had bought for a refit at Le Havre.

A bus crowded down the road packed with locals and top-heavy with produce. Young women paraded the street in colorful costumes with red flowers over their ears. Chinese, in black pajamas, pushed sweetmeat carts festooned with looking glasses and little bells. On the waterfront, out-islanders, like shrouded corpses, lay asleep in the shade of a shop's overhanging roof, waiting a passage to Saintes or Guadeloupe. A large pig broke loose and for a while all the available male population, and many females too, gave chase. A big schooner arrived from Guadeloupe and the deserted waterfront was immediately crowded. A German lady-tourist, her toenails painted red, wandered past the shipping. Beautiful, golden-skinned girls and boys, a mixture of French and Martiniquan, pedaled along on bicycles, the girls dressed in long white skirts and blouses, and were hailed from the ships by the dock. It is always painful to watch the life we are departing. At night, music from the bars floated down to the waterfront with the land wind.

The new delivery, *Zena*, was a 36-foot ketch, in fairly good order for a wooden boat that had been in tropical rain and sun, for the most part untended, for several years. The time came to sail; her lines were cast off, the anchor was broke out and off we went. I turned to wave farewell to the few acquaintances I had made during my three weeks in Martinique, when a black mass of cloud hid the sun. A hard rain-squall cracked down and sent *Zena* flying. Out through the pass we raced, out into the clear Caribbean beyond. A strong squall drove us deep into the water and like a wedge we split the confused sea outside. I turned around for a last look at Martinique on that visit, but the rain, like a curtain, had shut off the island.

Zena was one of the best monohulls I ever sailed. I forget where she was built or who was her designer, but I recall that she sailed like a witch. She needed to, for this was August, the middle of the hurricane season. No sooner had *Zena* strove out into the Atlantic Ocean north of the Virgin Island of St. Thomas than a storm broke. The winds blew and we flew before a southeaster which strained every rope and sail. During my sojourn in Martinique, I had rigged a rudimentary self-steering apparatus based on a design by Blondie Hasler. It had a huge wind-vane and it was not strong enough for the hardest steering, but in fair weather it worked fine, and allowed me to catch up on my sleep. Before a week was out we were off Cape Sable; she had reached the Banks; the land birds were left; gulls, haglets, petrels, ducks, had swum, dived or hovered around. No fisherman, she had passed the Banks; left three other sail well astern, far on the edge of the east at sundown, which was far to our west at dawn. Yet in running over these abysses far below whatever the dangers I was running into, I was running out of the risks, in these latitudes, of hundred of miles every day which have their own chances of squall, collision or, at that time of year, hurricane.

As for your own departures: when a skipper casts off mooring lines and departs, he does a splendid thing. When an anchor is weighed, it borders on the magnificent. He cuts himself off from the trammels of the land and starts for freedom and for the chance of things. He pulls the jibsail aweather (into the wind), he leans to her slowly pulling around, he sees the wind getting into the mainsail, and he senses that she feels the helm. He has her on a slant of wind, and he steers out between the marina or harbor piers. I am supposing, for the sake of good luck, that the wind is not blowing down the haven's mouth nor, for that matter, straight out of it. I am supposing, for the good luck of this venture, that in weighing anchor you have the wind so that you can sail it full and by (with the wind coming from a side) right past the marina walls, until you are well out into the tide outside.

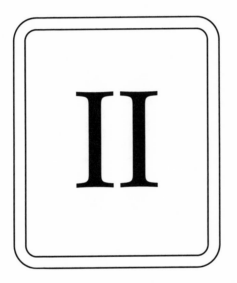

P A R T

II

A Day to Remember

The commemoration of D-Day, on June 6, 1944, as the main turning point of World War Two, leaves quite a few old sea dogs nonplussed. One fact stands clear: by June 6, 1944, the British and German navies had, day and night, hour by hour, in storm or calm, regardless of events on land, been at each others throats for over *four and a half years.*

Many suppose that getting to the Normandy beaches in early June of any year is much more convenient for politicians and their media entourages than reaching a remote spot way out in the stormy, grey Atlantic Ocean 600 miles from the nearest land. But that's where modern world history really hinged.

Apart from valid and honorable commemoration of the fallen, the over-playing of June 6 also rankles with anyone to do with the Red Army. Between June 1941 and D-Day in 1944, the U.S.S.R. lost millions of its soldiers and citizens to the Nazi invaders. It's true that much of the German initial success was due to the stupidity of Stalin's general staff purges during the 1930's, but no one can deny the superb victories of the Red Army, from September 1942, when it stopped the Panzer tanks stone-dead in their tracks at Stalingrad, until final victory was won in central Germany in May 1945.

But neither the mighty Red Army nor Britain could have prevailed if it had not been for supplies from North America, carried to them in ships which, across the Atlantic Ocean, ran a gauntlet of lurking wolf-packs of Nazi U-boats. Many failed.

Those that got through did so, until mid-1942, by the grace of God and mainly the British and Canadian Royal Navies. But before the U.S.S.R. was attacked, in the spring of 1941, there existed a more deadly menace to the Allies than even the U-boats: two *Kriegsmarine* battleships, *Bismarck* and *Tirpitz*.

For those who did not come of age before the advent of long-range air power and guided missiles, to understand the extent of the threat that, separately or acting together, these two Nazi battleships posed, two facts, then very real, must be appreciated: *any fleet is only as strong as its most powerful vessel*, and *as a threat, a "fleet in being" does not necessarily have to be put into action*. (Intercontinental missiles are an example of the latter.)

In May 1941, the deadly truths (known to the Admiralty in London) were that the most powerful ship in the British Navy, the freshly "completed" H.M.S. *Prince of Wales*, 38,000 tons, had four of her eight 15-inch guns not fully installed; the second most powerful British ship, H.M.S. *King George V* weighed also 38,000 tons and carried only 14-inch guns, while *Bismarck* and *Tirpitz* each weighed 50,000 tons and carried eight 15-inch guns. It was simple: the German Navy's biggest ships could steam faster, had bigger shells, could carry more of them and could fire more of them farther than any of the British Navy's biggest ships.

But there was more to it than mere size, speed, and fire power. Although now it would seem to us only common sense, the German Navy had introduced, into its latest ships, the new idea of damage control.

By 1941, the hulls of the latest-built German naval ships were divided up into many small watertight compartments. *Bismarck* had almost 200. The impact of a bomb, shell or torpedo explosion would be only on that one compartment. This system made *Bismarck* and *Tirpitz* the most *unsinkable* ships afloat. They were both built like steel honeycombs. On the other hand, British warships below decks but above water level, built for long cruises in the tropics—no air conditioning then—had mostly wide open spaces, from side to side and bow to stern.

For months, the British admirals had known that if either one of those two great German battleships broke loose from the fjords of Norway, it could, in the vast reaches of ocean then out of range of British land-based aircraft, dominate the sea lanes and destroy any Allied war or merchant vessel within thirty miles. The threat might throttle the British Isles into starvation, and within six weeks, force Winston Churchill, and whoever and whatever else could, to flee to Canada, and the successors to negotiate a surrender.

For Britain and her allies, the most dangerous time of World War Two was from May 24 until May 27, 1941, when *Bismarck*, having with one very accurate (or extremely lucky) shot sunk the lighter-armored British battle cruiser H.M.S. *Hood* off Iceland, was desperately attempting to reach a harbor on the Nazi-occupied west coast of France. If *Bismarck* had succeeded, she could have fueled and stored, well protected from British air strikes, for a far-ranging sortie, and with a dozen U-boats and a perhaps a couple of anti-aircraft escorts, *killed all trans-Atlantic sea traffic.*

Bismarck's threat wasn't merely the destruction of all Allied shipping and the potential starvation and consequent surrender of Britain. In those days, before the U.S. had built up its defenses or air forces, *Bismarck* could have held any of the cities on the Canadian or U.S. eastern seaboard or even the Panama Canal itself to ransom against a British (and even a U.S.) unconditional surrender. Imagine: a great, heavily armed, invulnerable, almost unsinkable ship carrying thousands of high explosive shells, which could be aimed in any direction for thirty miles, laying off the Verazzano Strait. There would have been absolutely nothing to effectively prevent *Bismarck* showing up off, say, Sydney Harbour, too.

As Germany and Italy's co-signatory of the anti-Comintern pact, Japan would not have needed, later that same year, to go to war with the U.S.; it could have achieved all its ambitions at no cost, simply by filling in the Far East power vacuum caused by the collapse of all of the European colonial powers.

At the start of World War Two, Germany had an excellent navy with good sailors and admirals, but judging from Hitler's immediate-post-*Bismarck* discarding of Germany's surface fleet, he did not fully understand sea-power as it was then.

On May 20, 1941, there had been a possibility that Hitler might extend his power world-wide to anywhere within thirty miles of any navigable seas (and that's where most humans lived). By midnight on May 27, 1941, that possibility was dead. By then there was a possibility—however remote— that a "D-Day" might eventually happen.

May 27, 1941 was the day when the Führer of the Thousand Year Reich found himself practically on his knees offering the Knight's Cross of the Iron Cross with Oak Leaves Cluster to *anyone* who could fix *Bismarck*'s rudder mechanism, jammed by a torpedo from a Royal Navy Fleet Air Arm aircraft launched from the British carrier H.M.S. *Ark Royal*. (Incidentally, only a month previously, Dr. Joseph Goebbels' Nazi Propaganda Ministry had declared "irrevocably" that *Ark Royal* had been sunk in the Mediterranean Sea.)

On May 24, 25, and 26, Hitler, in his messages to the German admirals, at first had threatened and ranted and fumed, then he'd whinged and whined, and finally he'd begged, as an ever-growing armada of British ships, all, except for *Prince of Wales*, with smaller armament than *Bismarck*, had chased after her, and then, as sore-wounded she circled, had gathered to close in on *Bismarck*.

Let me recall the names of some of those British ships: there were the carriers *Ark Royal* and *Victorious*. and also the battleships *King George V* and *Prince of Wales* and the slow First World War battleship *Rodney*. From the Rock of Gibraltar,

Britain's biggest aircraft-carrier *Victorious* raced out into the Atlantic Ocean along with a hastily assembled fleet of smaller ships known as *Force H*, but it never got within striking distance of *Bismarck* (carrier-borne aircraft range was only about 180 miles). There were, too, the cruisers *Norfolk* and *Suffolk*; they were both in at the start of the chase, and both hung on like bulldogs to *Bismarck*'s tail until the bitter end. Also, the elderly cruiser *Dorsetshire*, which at the very end of the battle, waddled up and with two salvoes of six 21-inch torpedoes each, finished off the flaming wreckage of what once had been the mighty *Bismarck*.

Give the *Kriegsmarine* its due, for an hour and more after all other firing had died, right until she capsized, one small gun blazed away from *Bismarck*. She didn't die easily at all. But I'm getting ahead . . .

Then there were the British destroyers, nine, if I recall rightly. They were the main close-attack craft for the *Bismarck* battle; to the admirals in London they were expendable against such a grand prize as securing Britain's ocean seaways from Hitler's surface threats. Without any doubt, in the hands of those nine destroyer-skippers, on the night of May 26 and 27, 1941, lay the destiny of anyone, of no matter what origin, who reads these words.

As *Prince of Wales* time and again advanced, retreated, all main guns blazing, steaming at 45 knots, and now and then held back just out of *Bismarck*'s firing range, the destroyers charged in at 50 knots, time after time, the whole night long, towards the end to within a few dozen meters of *Bismarck*, very often to come under point-blank fire from all *Bismarck*'s guns, to lob torpedoes, carefully aimed by line of sight, sometimes singly, sometimes in salvoes of six tin-fish each. All the while *Bismarck*'s guns roared in defiance.

Imagine, if you will, being on the bridge of one of those destroyers pelting at 30 knots over the high Atlantic ocean ridges, ramming and jolting, slithering and sliding through a watery, salt-spray-slashed blackness of night into a red glare of death gleaming from one end of the horizon to the other, as shells whoosh overhead and splash mightily every ten seconds or so . . . all around, ahead and astern of you . . .

After the battle, it was rumored that *Bismarck*, before she finally heeled over and sank, had sustained above water level hundreds of direct shell hits, and in her hull an incredible number of over one hundred torpedo strikes. Only a half dozen of *Bismarck*'s 2000 plus crewmen were picked up out of the heaving Atlantic seas. The British could not risk stopping for long and being in the periscope sights of a U-boat.

Hitler's first really serious mistake in World War Two was his neglect of long-range aircraft, especially as cover for *Bismarck* before she was ordered out into the Atlantic Ocean. Without absolute control of the North Atlantic Ocean, he could not subdue Britain nor threaten the U.S. Only three weeks after *Bismarck* went down, Hitler made his second most serious mistake: with Britain undefeated, he invaded the U.S.S.R. Seven months after *Bismarck*'s demise, Hitler made his third serious mistake: he declared war on the United States of America: an enemy which, with its bombers based in Britain, could attack him, but whose own country by then he couldn't reach.

When the VE Day fuss starts around May 8, let's save some whoopee for May 27, the anniversary of the moment on which really *was* hinged the fate of us all.

The Body

Among boating people, perhaps gathered in a bar, or a club-house, or even onboard, some subjects are never—or hardly ever—brought up in discussion. The reasons for this are many, but mostly I think it's because the likely occurrence is so rare as not to have been experienced by anyone present. In over fifty years at sea, of course, the number of unlikely things that have happened to me have been myriad, but one that seems to catch interest—perhaps even a morbid interest—when I mention it, which is very rarely, involves a dead body.

What do you do if you come across a human corpse afloat off a coast? Nowadays, when almost every cruising yacht is fitted with a radio transmitter, the answer is obvious and easy. You radio the local authorities and report your finding, then, if weather allows, await their arrival to pick up the body. If the weather doesn't allow you to hang about safely, you head into your destination and again report your finding's position when you arrive.

But in the old days, I'm talking about the 1950s, it wasn't so simple; but then nothing to do with boating was ever as simple as it is nowadays, despite the frequent moans of my contemporaries to the contrary. For one thing, we very rarely, if ever, had a radio transmitter. For another, before the days of "push-button navigation," we were very often unsure of our true position. And for another, in most countries—even those that are fairly well advanced now—the term "local authorities," as far as the sea was concerned, meant nothing. In the

Mediterranean, except for France and Italy, there were no properly-functioning "local authorities." Off Spain, the mere mention of it would have been considered as a joke. The list of differences between sailing then and now could go on and on.

In 1955, I was making a northing passage from Gibraltar to Monaco. I was in the last leg of delivering, solo, a very sweet-sailing 36-footer from her builder's yard in Holland to her new owner. He was a Mexican, who for some reason had given his boat an Irish name, *Shindig*. I'd started off from Den Helder in Holland in late September and had a regular beat down Channel, then out into the open ocean, and so on the wind into Gibraltar. That had taken about two weeks. In those days, we didn't usually have automatic steering gear or wind-vanes; and those that existed were not dependable. So a longish trip such as Holland to Gibraltar meant many, many hours at the tiller, with snatches of sleep as and when they might be taken. It was hard going, and we delivery skippers earned our money, believe me, every measly penny of it.

Three days on the Rock resting, re-stocking food and water (few fridges then!), and there we were, *Shindig* and I, off the coast of Spain, about thirty miles southwest of the island of Ibiza. It's almost always good sailing in that area in the autumn. It's not too warm for comfort, what wind there is can come from anywhere, but it's rarely too blustery and there were always the fantastic views of the mountain range of the Sierra Nevada to the north to while away the hours becalmed; to the south was the blue haze of the mountains of Algeria.

It was just before dusk when I sighted the body. There wasn't much breeze and I was quite tired. Then, on the slowly heaving, dappled waters ahead, I sighted a shape. At first I thought it might be a dead dolphin, for they drown, too, just like people, and are given up again by the sea. It was a human body. As usual when the sea gives up its dead, it was bloated. As *Shindig* bore down on it, I could see that it was a male—for some reason I thought youngish—and that he had fair hair.

The sea and the birds had been at work on his head, so his features were not clear, to say the least. I felt a strange pity for him and decided to try to get him into port for a decent burial. He was dressed in a whitish shirt and black pants. There were very few "tourists" in the '50s. I got the idea, somehow, that he was a merchant seaman who had perhaps fallen overboard from his ship. I hove to and drifted down on the corpse. Holding my nose (easy for me, I've a big one), I slung a line around his belt, then under his arms, and so yoked, I towed him astern, head first, and made in, at about two knots, for Ibiza Harbor, which I already knew, and where I had friends.

The winds that night were weak or contrary, as they mostly are when you're anxious to reach port. From dawn until noon next day I watched the fortressed hill above Ibiza Town creep closer and closer, until at last, in the early afternoon, I reached the harbor and tied up under the sea wall. A small knot of fisher lads had seen the body trailing astern of *Shindig* and before long two Civil Guard officers were on the jetty, ordering me away. I explained to them (my Spanish was fair) that I had found the body out at sea and brought it in for a Christian burial, but to no avail. "How do we know he is a Christian?" they asked. Gingerly, they searched the body's clothes for papers—there were none.

"You must take the body to Majorca, to Palma," the sergeant ordered, as his colleague laboriously wrote down all the details of the affair. "We will report your approach to the authorities there," he added.

This was long before the days of mass tourism in Spain. In those days, no one argued with their Civil Guard, and so off *Shindig* and I went, on our way again, bound eighty miles northeast for Majorca.

To cut a long story sideways, the story was repeated in Palma, then in Andraitx, a small port on the southwest tip of Majorca, and then I had to sail for the Spanish mainland, for Alicante. All of this took five days; all the time the body trailing astern was deteriorating seriously, and the stench meant that I had to lengthen the towing line, until by the time I was thrown out of Alicante it was all of three hundred feet long. The superstitious Spanish fishermen, having heard of the crazy foreign sailor with his corpse, were avoiding my boat like the plague. All the way from Alicante to Barcelona, off each and every port, no matter how small, a fishing boat was sent out to *Shindig* to warn me off.

Finally, in Barcelona, even then a big cosmopolitan seaport, with the body by then almost falling to bits, ten days after I had found it, and allowed only to anchor for twenty-four hours, I headed, under Civil Guard escort, for the British Consulate. I told them that I would tow the corpse no more. The Consulate officials, although there was no indication that the body was British (but did it matter?) went to work on the Port Authorities. The Port Captain came to our aid and ordered his Spanish Navy men to take the corpse off my hands and give it a decent burial at a Protestant graveyard somewhere near the mountain of Montjuich. I had to borrow a black suit and go along to the funeral, a real Mediterranean affair, with four black horses wearing black plumes. The British Consul and I were the only mourners. I never liked leaving a job half-done.

A few years later I met the Barcelona British Consul again. By that time he was retired. He told me that he had made enquiries through Lloyd's of London, the shipping agents, about anyone missing from ships, and that the general appearance of the corpse agreed with that of an engineer who had been lost from an Argentinian ship which had passed through the area where I had discovered the corpse, only a week or so before. The Consul had informed the Spanish officials, an exhumation had been ordered and positive identification had been made. The drowned officer had been an Argentinian-Catalan Catholic who had emigrated from Spain to Buenos Aires with his family as a boy. He had been born in Barcelona . . . only a stone's throw away from the Catholic cemetery where he was reburied and now rests.

Which leads me sometimes to wonder: is there perhaps a schematic reason for all things—even bigotry, superstition, and bureaucratic delay? Is perhaps everything *connected*, no matter how stupid or futile it seems?

EPISODE 12

The Steamer Scarer

Creasey was a big, balding man who usually wore thick woolen jerseys and walked with an ambling gait. He and his little sloop were well known on the coast of Yorkshire, and even farther afield, in the '50s. I knocked around that area myself for a couple of months, while I was waiting to deliver to Gibraltar the first of two ketches being built in Hartlepool. Yorkshire was full of fine folk, the meals were hearty, the beer in the Red Lion waterfront inn, at Whitby, where I stayed, was excellent, the rooms were cheap and the maid Rosie was a charming, amenable lass. What more could a shore-bound delivery skipper want?

When I'd first met him, Creasey struck me as being cold. Standoffishness is not a Yorkshire characteristic; people in the Red Lion put it down, in Creasey's case, to his being a solicitor; what in the States is called an attorney. They were all said to be failed barristers, and so they were expected to be bloody-minded.

In England, a regular customer's absence in a pub is soon noticed. After I'd not seen Creasey hanging about for a day or two, I enquired about him; someone told me he'd taken off with his wife for a summer cruise to Denmark, across the North Sea. It wasn't the calmest stretch of saltwater on planet Earth, nor the warmest, but when you were accustomed to hard winds and cold it wasn't too bad.

In those days, before the advent of small, cheap, electronic navigation aids, any trip in a small craft from the coast

78

of Britain to anywhere in continental Europe was looked upon by most people as quite an adventure. I suppose it still is—the weather's about the same—but nowhere is it considered near as much an adventure now as it was then. A trip across the North Sea then was, for most British yachtsmen, the apex of venturesome voyaging. The skies were mostly overcast, the tides were strong, there were sand banks and shoals everywhere, and the wind was likely to come from any direction and blow its head off.

When I returned to Yorkshire the following spring from the sunny Rock to collect the second ketch, of course the first place I made for was the Red Lion in Whitby. Rosie was still there, still smiling, still available; hair the color of corn, eyes sea-green.

Creasey was in his usual corner of the saloon bar. Imagine my surprise when he sent me over a pint of beer. I was playing darts at the time. I was a dab-hand at darts then . . . won many a pint.

"It's all right, Taff," said my opponent. "Old Creasey's lost his missus—he's gone a bit off his rocker . . ."

They call all Welshmen "Taff" in Yorkshire. But fair's fair, and so, although I wasn't anxious for Creasey's company, I wandered over and thanked him for the pint. "Sorry to hear about your wife," said I.

Creasey looked down at me and smiled. For the first time I saw that his eyes were that startling light Saxon-blue seen only, it seemed, around the shores of the North Sea. I suddenly realized that he was a very lonely man. We talked about my trip to Gibraltar—it'd been a roughish one across the Bay of Biscay.

I was just about to leave Creasey's company. "Have another beer, old chap," he offered, and before I could refuse there was a second pint sitting in front of me. Of course, I got stuck into it. I liked my ale in those days.

Creasey gave a nervous cough. "Look," he said, "look here . . . I've something on my mind." He stared around the smoky pub vault, then his gaze again shyly met mine. "I can't talk about it with these people. You've done an awful lot of sailing . . . perhaps you can, as it were, well . . . give me some idea . . . " His voice trailed off.

"Only if you let me buy you a drink," I interjected; there was only a half-hour until closing time, then Rosie would be waiting. Reluctantly I settled down to hear Creasey's tale.

"Clare . . . my wife, you know . . . was quite a good sailor, although she did suffer from seasickness for the first few hours out whenever we went out in any kind of weather . . . On the way over to Esbjerg, she said she felt a bit woozy now and then. Of course, we're . . . were . . . both getting on a bit in years, so we thought little of it. We were within sight of Esbjerg Harbor when she collapsed. The Danes were very good about the whole thing, and had her into hospital in a twinkling. I went with her in the ambulance, but an hour after we arrived she . . . passed away."

"I'm sorry," I said, feeling, as always at the mention by someone who had been close to someone now dead, whom I hardly knew when alive, more embarrassed than anything else.

"Well, I was . . . cut up. You may imagine. Thirty-five years married . . . " Creasey stirred his drink and stared at the floor for a moment. "Anyway," he went on, "I waited around for the funeral, and then sailed off again to get back to England and clear up my wife's estate, that kind of thing. I was in an . . . emotional state . . . I can tell you. But luckily the weather was quite fine and I managed the boat all right on my own. For the first afternoon, it blew quite hard, then it went down during the night, and the second day I'd no wind at all, and motored to pick up sight of the coast—it's what, two hundred miles? The evening of the second day, the fog just clamped down. It was so thick that at times I couldn't see my own bow."

I nodded my head. I knew the hazards of fog all right.

Creasey swigged his drink. "It must have been about

midnight. I was heading northeast very slowly with the motor ticking over and the fog like a blanket all around me. I'd heard this siren noise—obviously a ship—and I was really wary; there was no way I could tell where it was coming from . . . All I knew was that it was getting louder and louder and nearer and nearer . . . and then, right out of the fog, right in front of my bow, there was this monstrous black shadow . . . as big as a . . . courthouse . . . I can tell you it frightened the living daylights out of me . . . "

I grinned at Creasey. I knew that feeling well. I raised my eyebrows in an unspoken question.

He went on, "Well, of course I dived down into the cabin and grabbed the floodlight—you know, the old steamer scarer. I held it out clear of everything and switched it on. The beam was like a solid bar of shining silver as it cut through the fog. I shined it right onto the steamer's bridge. I even saw, in the reflection of the beam, a man come out on the signal deck and shield his eyes with his forearm. The steamer changed course right then, right in front of my bow. She must have missed me by no more than a yard."

The pub landlord sang out, "Time, gentlemen, please!" We had ten minutes left to finish our drinks.

"You were lucky," I observed, as Creasey drained his glass. His eyes met mine again. There was something in them close to madness.

"Yes, I was, wasn't I?" he half-grinned. "But there had been a . . . problem . . . with the electrics on the way to Esbjerg, and I'd . . . disconnected the floodlight from the battery, while I fixed it . . . and I'd forgotten, what with the funeral and every-thing . . . to reconnect it. I didn't think about it at all until the steamer had passed by safely and disappeared. Then I . . . well, I just sort of stood there stupidly for a minute, until I pulled on the floodlight cable, and there were the ends, the battery ends. There they were, loose, not connected to anything . . . I switched on the floodlight . . . the steamer scarer . . . then and there, to try it again. Of course it was as dead as a dodo . . .

Then I sighted the buoy off Spurn Head, and decided I'd dreamed the whole thing and thought no more about it."

People around us were donning their hats and coats and drifting off out through the oaken pub doors into the rain outside.

"Well," I said to comfort Creasey, "that's happened to me a few times, I mean where I've been so tired I've imagined that things have happened that never have . . . and you . . . with an emotional upheaval and everything . . . " I trailed off.

The pub was almost empty now. Rosie, behind the bar, winked at me as she cleared up the glasses. She was a little darling, that one. I was doing my best not to give our game away to Creasey.

Creasey grabbed my arm. "No, but you see . . . I got into Kingston that same night—still in a fog, but clearing—and tied up at the commercial wharf. The next day I slept until about noon—I was tired out, you see—and was wakened by a voice calling the name of my boat from the jetty. I popped my head up, and there was this ship's officer standing there, in uniform. "Good afternoon, and what can I do for you?" I said.

"'Recognized your boat from last night!' the officer shouted at me as I stared at him. He was a youngish chap; Norwegian, I presumed from his accent. 'I couldn't mistake you with that yellow dinghy on your deck! We almost hit you! I rushed out on the side-bridge. I wasn't sure you were there until you flashed that light at us. My God, it almost blinded me. Of course, I ordered to change course right away!'"

Creasey's eyes were half-closed. "All I could do was thank the chap," he whispered. He looked up and smiled, "But I mustn't keep you . . . only I can't help wondering . . . "

Rosie was signaling me from the back of the bar. It was time for me to return to my room. I made some excuse and left Creasey staring at me, standing alone at the bar of the empty pub-vault. I was sailing for Gibraltar next day, and that was the last I ever saw of him.

EPISODE 13

The Cradle Song

The Mediterranean wind frequently doesn't blow with a regular force, as it mostly does in other climes. It pulses. It's bitchy. One minute it's down to fifteen knots, the next minute comes a bluster, anything up to thirty or forty knots or more. It needs a lot of attention. You have to have eyes and ears in your elbows. You have to concentrate all the time. It's not easy sailing in the Mediterranean at night with a full gale blowing all the way from Vesuvius. With a badly beaten-up woman below, and another screaming her head off, my own head was too full of concerns for me to say anything much to Antonio for a minute or two . . .

I stared at the incredible scene in *Creswell*'s cabin for a moment. It was truly horrifying. Over *Creswell*'s smashing, jerking, crashing deck I headed back for the bilge pump and desperately heaved away at the great brass handle until the pump got a suction. From then on it was "Armstrong's Patent"—pump, pump, and more pump. Half the night Antonio and I spelled each other at the heavy pump and the heaving wheel, as the wind rose to full storm force and piled up frenetic seas in their millions over the mile-wide, shallow bank under the strait.

After I'd pumped out about a ton of seawater which had sluiced onboard, I checked out the cabin again. The scene topsides was bad enough, but below, in the ghostly light of the oil lamp, purposely kept dim so as to preserve our night vision, it was a view of horror. By now Sissie had managed to get about a quarter of the gin down the heaving, lashing *señora*, so at least her screams were a little less terrifying. It looked as if Sissie had had a slug, too—there was a gleam of determination in her eyes now that brought to mind Karsh's portrait of Churchill glowering.

"Deah Skippah!" she crowed, "what a topping ideah of yours! Ai've managed to give *dahling* Miss Pomeroy a teeny drop, too! The poor deah is in a *frightful fret*. I think Señora Puig is feeling a weeny bit better, now!"

"Good," I shouted back at her, as Nelson gazed damply up from under the table in abject misery. "I'm not letting her husband down here. I don't want any panic. It's obvious he loves her far too much to help her a great deal. You stay with her. Try to get a little bit more gin into her—not too much. And for God's sake, make some cocoa or something! We need cheering up, lass—death's abroad! There's only us and the gin to stove its bloody face in!" Then I recovered myself and subdued my Welshness. It's not much help when the English are determined. "Did you read that thing about a-borning in *Reed's*?" I asked her.

"Ai'm trying to. It's jolly difficult in this light. Can we turn the lamp up a little?"

"No, take the book over to the stove when you boil the water—and for Chrissake, be careful!" Then I staggered back on deck to relieve Antonio after another fifteen minutes of wild pumping. All heavy work.

By two o'clock we had smashed our way another fifty yards or so to the east against the bitter wind. At two-fifteen Sissie appeared on deck and leaped down into the cockpit besides me. "Oh, *deah*, she's in heavy labor!" The water streamed off Sissie's thin, frilly blouse, and the tears streamed from her eyes.

I was too astounded to say anything for a moment. I stared at Sissie, squinting against the flailing rain and lashing spray, and gritted my teeth. Then I made up my mind. I would have to stop this almost hopeless fray with the storm and head *with* the wind. Our argument with the Fates was far too futile. They would never accede to our powerful demands and our puny strength. We were being too big for our boots.

"I'm wearing her around, Sissie. It'll take all night and tomorrow forenoon to buck this bloody strait!"

I started to move the wheel around to pass *Creswell*'s bow away from the raging wind. Slowly the boat obeyed me. Antonio nodded his head as he eased the mainsheet. He had already figured out my intentions. Sissie stood by the jib sheet, ready to pay it out a touch. Then, as the noise of the wind and sea lessened while *Creswell* disdainfully turned her back on them, there was a particularly dreadful howl from down below. I half-pushed Sissie toward the cabin, and concentrated on the helm. It's not an easy maneuver, wearing off in a full storm.

"I'm making for the west coast of Ibiza, Antonio. I'm going to seek shelter in the lee or get her around to San Antonio!" This was a small port and holiday resort on the northwest side of Ibiza island. "We can get her to a doctor there!"

The weather, now that we were running away from it, was far less violent. *Creswell* retreated to the west into the black nothingness of the night . . .

From the strait to Es Vedra, on the southwest tip of Ibiza, was about fourteen miles. Off the wind, on a dead run, still with all sail up, *Creswell* flew, her stern yawing this way and that, more or less on an even keel now, but rearing and pitching like a maddened steer. Antonio and I still fought the stiff pump and struggling helm.

By five o'clock, in the murky light of a rain-ripped gray sky, weary by now, only kept ataut by Sissie's cocoa and the screams of Señora Puig, we sighted, about a quarter of a mile away, the great conical rock of Es Vedra, almost a thousand feet high, huge and ghostly as it reared up to the low black clouds, straight from the seabed. We knew there might be hope for us in this insane night . . .

Then it happened.

I somehow knew it was going to happen. It wasn't a case of calculating the likelihood. It was more an instant pre-science. The stern smashed down on the far edge of the rock just as we were about to clear the danger, miraculously, so we had thought, scot-free. The rudder hit the rock, the shock broke the rudder cable bottle-screws, and the rudder, being re-movable, jumped off its pintles.

The rudder was secured to the hull by a rope lanyard about six feet long, so we didn't lose it; but we were, in effect, rudderless. It would be extremely hazardous, even foolish with the boat bouncing around as she was, to try to lean over the whaleback stern and recover the rudder. There were more pressing demands, to say the least.

It isn't often, thank all the gods, that a sailor finds himself out in a raging gale, with a possibly damaged keel, and rud-derless, with an agonized, hysterical pregnant woman below, screaming blue murder, another one so badly beaten up that she can hardly see, and another who has never had any mid-wifery training.

I didn't need to tell Antonio. He pulled me to the wheel, cast off all the sheets, levitated himself somehow to the foot of the wildly swinging mainmast, and let go the jib, the gaff, and the main halyard. The mainsail came down with a clatter as Antonio scrabbled at the terylene and dragged the flailing sail down onto the coachroof. It was a performance which would have made a Chinese acrobat look like an undertaker.

With the boat almost stopped in the crazily heaving seas, I could now leave the wheel and rescue the rudder. Soon, after panting and moaning for ten minutes, stretched right over the bouncing, narrow whaleback stern, I somehow managed to wangle the gudgeons of the eighty-pound rudder over the pintles on the pounding and lunging sternpost, re-screw the steering cables, and regain command of the boat.

Within minutes of getting underway again, *Creswell* had zoomed beyond Es Vedra rock. Quite suddenly, as the rock loomed over us, very close, there was no more wind, no more panicky seas. It was as though the storm had never been. *Creswell* was one minute yawing, pounding, rising, and falling like a startled stag; the next minute upright, sedate, and slowing. Now almost the only noises were the loud groans and sobs of Señora Puig below . . .

The groans coming from down below were heart-rending, nerve-shattering—almost soul-destroying. It was horrible. I could not think of anything that sounded more terrifying since the berg had almost capsized onto *Creswell* in the Arctic five years before. The screams were truly dreadful to hear. Now Antonio broke down. He bent his head forward and burst out sobbing.

I leaned over and clutched his shoulder. "Come on, Antonio, we'll leave the mess below. Let's get underway again. We can be in San Antonio by eight." It was now dawn. Idleness is no cure for grief.

No sooner had Antonio dragged himself to his feet again, still sobbing, when another sound came from down below. It was not a high-pitched scream now; not a low, agonized moan; not a bellow of pain. It was thin but quite loud—loud enough to echo back from the almost vertical sides of the great rock only a few yards away from the bedraggled *Creswell*. This voice yelled and gurgled. It screamed protest, it demanded justice, it hollered violent indignation. For a moment Antonio and I stood, quite close to one another, staring in disbelief into each other's eyes.

"*No lo creo!* I don't believe it . . . " murmured Antonio. Then he grabbed the mainsheet horse-rail and swung himself over it. "*Un chiquito*? A boy?" he shouted . . .

All our bone-weariness completely forgotten, Antonio and I were crowding the companionway hatch. I peered down at the mess below. Sissie was standing, still wet through, her breasts heaving under the now dirty and bedraggled frilly blouse. In her arms, she held a bundle wrapped in one of my shirts. Her face beamed.

La Pomeroy somehow squeezed past us, a bucket in hand. Antonio rushed down the ladder, and tried to grab the bundle from Sissie, but she wouldn't let go. "Skippah, tell him to be careful!"

I didn't need to. Antonio sensed that he was not in order, and poked one of his calloused fingers into the bundle. Now he was cooing too. Behind him again now, Miss Pomeroy, all bashed and battered, took the hands of a weakly smiling, silent Señora Puig. Then Antonio looked down at his wife, reached for her, and broke into great, deep sobs.

By this time I had managed to drag myself down the ladder and take a peek at the tiny face. It wasn't very handsome. It looked a bit like a walnut, all creases and little wrinkles— rather like a miniature version of Miss Pomeroy's. The tiny lad's eyes were open. Sissie told me later that he couldn't see yet, but he looked at me and I could swear he winked. Then he stared at me for a few seconds longer, wondering just what kind of world he had entered. He gazed into my salt-be-grimed, sleep-begging, filthy, bearded face, curled his little mouth up, frowned, and let out a bellow which I told Sissie would be heard in Gibraltar.

"He's going to be a big, strong fisherman," cooed Sissie. "Aren't you, oh you adorable little cheppie."

"More like a bloody cattle-boat skipper, with a voice like that," said I.

Now Antonio was on his knees, praying. In his hands he held his wife's rosary. As I turned and started up the ladder to get the sails up and head for San Antonio with our new passenger, I noticed Sissie's hands. Both were scalded and blistered by hot water from the fallen kettle.

That's how Antonio Cecilio Tristan Vedra Pomeroy Creswell Puig of Formentera received his name.

Previously published in *Seagulls in My Soup* (1991)

The Psychology of an Adventurer

The point at which explorers and ocean-solo-sailors meet on common ground is that in general they have all or some of the following characteristics:

The first is a consuming *curiosity* —the need to know what is beyond the horizon, beyond the next hill or bend in the track.

The second (and I shall probably dodge brickbats for this from some explorers) is what at first might seem to be an overweening *egoism*. Solo-sailors and explorers are, in the main, extremely individualistic. But with the passage of years, this is modified through certain risks and suffering which we sometimes are forced to endure.

The third attribute is a *stubbornness*—an almost illogical refusal to accept "impossible" odds.

The fourth characteristic is a kind of *pride*; not so much in achievement, but in the fact that they *set out*. The achievement of an aim is not necessarily, in itself, the be-all and end-all of everything to us. Indeed, for some expeditions, many important discoveries have been made which were not foreseen when the aims of the venture were set. To reach the target is not as important as to *survive*, even if failure to attain the goal is incurred.

The fifth attribute is a strange sort of *patriotism*. It is not a xenophobic disdain for people of another ilk, nor a mindless waving of a flag—it is more a patriotism of a peer group. It is as if sailors and explorers share a mystical experience with each other, which only they can appreciate. And so they do, indeed, for a person who has clung to the blizzard-swept ledges of Annapurna has much in common with a person who has hammered off the Horn. For my part, it's impossible for me to consider, for example, Bernard Moitessier as a French- man, or Slocum, Peary or Lindbergh as Americans, and I *never* think of Nansen, Amundsen and Heyerdahl as Norwegians; I think of them as Explorers—they belong to the whole world.

The sixth attribute is a *competitiveness*, and yet again this is of a special nature. It is not the same type of competitiveness which is seen in commerce or in the general run of sports. It is not to bring someone else down—not to beat another—and when it has been it has almost always led to disaster (witness Scott's race against Amundsen for the Pole). The mood is more toward adding another human achievement, more a competition with the forces of nature.

The seventh attribute, and the one most alluded to by sedentary cynics, is a *death-wish*. I myself have observed it in several young people, some of whom, in the course of time, had their wish granted. But in the sailors and explorers of any experience whom I have encountered, and especially the solo ocean-sailors, including Sir Francis Chichester, Sir Alec Rose, Frank Casper, Robin Knox-Johnston, Bernard Moitessier, Naomi James, Clare Francis and many, many more, I have never heard them express anything remotely like a death- wish. It may, in some cases, have been there, but if it was, it was very well hidden.

In this subject—the psychology of adventure—it is im- possible for me to be objective. As for my own exploratory en- deavors—many of my older listeners will have realized that many things happen in the course of their lives, which at the time they happen do not seem to make much sense, nor to have much significance. It is only after a matter of time— sometimes of years—that we realize where a specific piece of the great puzzle fits into the eventual scheme of things. So it was in my case.

I commenced small-craft voyaging in 1953. In 1959, I set off for the Arctic to attempt to sail the farthest north. It was not until I emerged from the ice-pack in 1961, after over fifteen months of isolation and deprivation, that I began to realize into what mold fate was casting me. Even then it was all very vague (I saw no blinding light), and it was a few more years until I recognized fully that I had been, for several years, *exploring the limits of human endurance*, mostly in solitude until then.

The great query which, unknown to me, had been asked, was: what are the limits of endurance of one person, unsupported, unsponsored, mainly isolated from his fellow beings? *What are the limits of lone endurance?*

Much later—over a decade later, when notice of my activities reached the general public, I was accused by a few critics of madness and/or machismo and a few other more esoteric, more exotic faults. If I had intentionally set out in the first place to explore the limits of lone endurance, I would have agreed with them, but that was not the case. I was maneuvered into my field of exploration by forces which can only be guessed at. It is as if I were some tiny part of a much greater design.

I was also accused of being "anachronistic"'of being born too late. The critics proclaimed that "the age of heroes is over." I have never put myself forward as a hero. Neither the seas, nor the ice, nor the jungle produces "heroes" in the sense meant by the critics—only the popular media can do that. As for anachronism, I fail to see how anyone who uses modern materials, and who tries to keep himself informed of all the latest developments in design and materials, can be that. Not only materials, but also the stresses which they are able to endure.

But what about the stresses which humans can endure? To what limits can a person drive him/herself? What effects do unrelieved hardship and continual deprivation have on a person mentally, physically and spiritually? In isolation? Alone?

Monitored experiments and investigations into this question might—almost certainly would—lead to false deductions and conclusions by the fact that even if the subject were being observed instrumentally, even if he/she were isolated geographically, the very knowledge that he or she was being observed would change his or her every attitude.

A simpler retort to my critics might have been: given that my field of endeavor was to explore the limits of human endurance, *alone*, could I expect someone else to endure in my place, and whom could I ask?

The human body and psyche, in general, and with a modicum of luck by way of good health and little ill-treatment (self-inflicted or otherwise) and accidents, are capable of great adjustments to circumstances. Barring unavoidable sickness and extreme age, the limits of human endurance seem to me to be much greater than is generally presumed to be the case. I have not yet found them, although in some directions I must have been pretty close to them.

On the question of aging. One of the paradoxes of the human condition is the fact that as our bodies deteriorate in the natural process of aging, so our minds *should* become wiser. Here the small-craft sailor has something of an advantage, most of the time, over the land-explorers. Physical strength to a small craft sailor is important at times, but rarely is it more important than skill and knowledge.

When the physical demands of our activity become too much for us to perform with reasonable efficiency, the fact must be accepted. Then is the time to ease up physically and to apply the wisdom and skills of a lifetime to teaching others who will follow. Whatever we do, we must learn to accept gracefully the limitations imposed upon us by age or accident. We must not begrudge nature her course; and in return she will bequeath to us the ability to pass on our knowledge. The underlying cause of senility is *resentment* against death.

As far as death is concerned, the fear of natural death, that is, the final phase in the life process, is unreasonable. The litmus test of that statement is for me to ask which of you, offered the opportunity, would, after thinking about it *deeply*, choose to remain alive forever? My attitude to the prospect of untimely death is very different, I suppose, to many other folks. I have been many times extremely close to death by accident or disaster and even human evil intent, and on each and every occasion, once I had passed through the bog-swamp of fear (a quicker passage each time), my most salient reaction was, "What a bloody fool I am to get myself into this situation!"

The two most formidable enemies of the solo-explorer, and indeed, I think, of all of us, are *fear* and *loneliness*, and either one can be the result of the other. Unless we are very wary, either one can give birth to panic, with dire, often fatal, results.

Loneliness is very different to solitude. I can be much more "lonely" in the middle of Times Square, surrounded by thousands of other human (and some perhaps not-so-human) beings, and yet not "lonely" in the far reaches of the ocean, perhaps more than a thousand miles from the nearest other human.

The defeat of loneliness is a stringent self-operation. It involves peeling off all our inherited and learned defense mechanisms and looking at our condition as it really is and recognizing that we are, all of us, alone in the vastness of the Universe from the moment we are born until the second we die, and that all social intercourse, of whatever nature, is but an attempted disguising of this fact. A sometimes *poetic*, sometimes *pitiful*, sometimes *beautiful*, sometimes *ugly*, sometimes *deadly serious* and sometimes *hysterically hilarious* disguise, but none the less a disguise. We must learn by conscious effort of the paradox of human alone-ness and togetherness at the same time, and so learn to appreciate *solitude*.

In solitude, we can learn about ourselves as well as about others. In solitude, we can appreciate every occurrence, every phenomenon, every thought, every discovery; each one magnified in perception and experience to an extent undreamable to those who have not lived in complete solitude for any length of time.

Fear is the most animalistic part of our nature. Where there is violence and stupidity, where there is resentment and cruelty, where there is greed and self-pity, there is fear. Fear is the nether side of reason, which must be coldly rationalized out of our psyches. Fear interferes with the process of solving problems. Some people will tell us that fear is a natural emotional reaction to circumstances, that it is part of human nature, but I will respond that so is courage, and courage, to me, is merely the ability, the presence of mind, to realize that fear is the deadly opposite of reason.

There are ways to ease the assaults of loneliness, pain and fear. The human intellect, well nurtured, can resist and defeat these emotions, but just as important as intelligence and courage, and surely a necessary adjunct to them, are a sense of humor, and a belief in a rhythm, a design, a logic, in the cosmic scheme of things. Call it Allah, Jehovah, God, or what you will.

Some people, if they knew that I talk to myself when I am alone at sea, might think that I am a little crazy. Most single-handers I have met have assured me that they do this, too. Doctor Lilley, a few years back, carried out a study on solo sailors, a psychological study, to find out just how "nutty" we really are. Lilley has come to a simple conclusion: that ocean solo sailors *must* be sane because a mentally disturbed person *by definition* cannot cross an ocean alone. True, there have been some "crazies" who have had more than their share of luck, but anyone who is not completely sane would be highly likely to make serious errors of judgment and of navigation. In heavy weather, he would be very likely to break down completely.

We sailors know that the amount of physical and mental stress which we have endured when the ocean weather had really let loose is enough at times to tempt us to drop on our knees and weep and plead to God—and the devil, if need be, for cessation and safety; for just one infinitesimal moiety of comfort, one more, before we are beaten into the void of an unknown death. That we haven't done this, that we have resisted the temptation to do it, even when hope is but one last ragged thread stretched to the breaking limit, is our earned badge of sanity.

After a pitchpoling hell of brute violence out in the ocean, we listen askance to the landsmen's plaints of woe. To us a broken down hot water heater or a ten-cent increase in the price of gasoline soon find their place in our scheme of priorities.

But even when things are at their worst at sea, we rarely wish to be anywhere else than where we are at that blessed moment, apart, perhaps, from being with our loved ones. That, usually, is my only regret. As for being away from the land, it is very often good to be away from it all; the crowding; the juggling for money and position and power . . . out there, whatever the drawbacks, there is none of that. As far as the sea is concerned, there are only two positions; only two levels, afloat and under, and the sea doesn't care a hoot which level we are on. As for money at sea, we know that when the going gets rough, or when we are becalmed and watch our precious freshwater supply slowly sink, it wouldn't matter if our boat's keel had been cast out of solid gold and her winches were made of pure platinum, and if we owned all the oil fields of Arabia, it simply would make not one whit of difference to the sea, because she doesn't care.

When it is time for me to delve into myself, into my own motivations, I find my own self-significance has little place in them. Looking for my own self-significance might have had much to do with my making my own first voyages; I was much more "romantic" then (naturally), but now my significance matters less and less as time goes by. I know I am of interest to a few publishers, and I suppose, to my agent, and to some of my readers, but I don't imagine that they would go into paroxysms of grief if I should fail to come back to shore. More likely the publishers would have a field day publicizing my non-reappearance and issuing another edition of my books—and good luck to them.

Like most other people, I suppose, I ask myself about fame. I came to the conclusion long ago that I would rather make something worthwhile to leave behind me: books, a record of my life and observations, and be comparatively unknown, than make nothing of real use to anyone and be famed.

Curiosity I can now discount, too. I suppose there was something new on every day of every voyage that I ever made; I would have been surprised if there wasn't—that in itself would have been a curiosity.

The need for independence is a different matter. Retaining my independence—the control of my own destiny—that is very important indeed to me. There are too many people leaning on other people nowadays. I would literally rather starve to death than to have to depend on someone else to guide my future.

I do not consider that when I depart for sea I am escaping from a society that I do not agree with, or that does not agree with me. I can fit in practically anywhere and I am old enough now to be able to make allowances for what I see as other people's failings; and hope they will do the same for me. Besides, anyone who imagines that going to sea in a small boat on a long voyage is an escape is either a fool or simply does not know any better.

Physically, life ashore is much easier than it is at sea. So many things are done and provided for the landsman that most of the time he does not even think about, much less appreciate. At sea, we are our own grocer, water-supplier, cook, doctor, dentist, fireman, policeman, engineer, navigator; there we are—King, President, and Prime Minister, all rolled into one, in our own little States. But on our "desks" the buck not only stops—it starts, too.

Adventurousness, of course, is part of our nature. The sense of all the limitless space out there; the out-witting of all the mighty forces ranged against us, the out-guiling of storms and calms and currents and even the passage of time itself, the careful rolling of the dice each time the odds are raised against us; all these spice my sense of adventure. Without that sense I am sure, that for me at least, life could not be lived to its fullest extent.

Of course, the "psychiatrist's couch crowd" will make noises about "masochism" and all kinds of other nonsense, but they will rarely admit that sometimes a hard struggle, with a dose of fear thrown in for good measure, is the best medicine ever concocted for man or beast.

As for competitiveness, although it exists in me to some degree, I do not thirst at the brim of the great silver race winner's cup. I have only taken part in three races in my life and on each occasion it was merely to help out friends. By nature I am not competitive with other humans. Perhaps it is that most of my competitive spirit over the past two and a half decades has been pitted and spent so much against the forces of nature. The sea and the weather are my real competitors.

Competition, I suggest, is one of the stumbling blocks of shore-side experience. The only valid competition is in the gaining of a mate. There is too much trying to out-do, to beat others, and not enough trying to relate to one another. To me the contention that competition with others brings out the best is only a half-truth, because often a person's "best" is not always the best for others; sometimes it is not even best for himself.

True, at sea, in a solo race, it is somewhat different. Here one is isolated from the other competitors, so we can rarely actually harm them, but if we let ruthless ambition go to our heads, we may surely allow the sea to harm us, through our own foolhardiness or downright blind stupidity. The reason that other creatures, especially the sea-creatures, survive, is that they do not, except in gaining a mate, compete with each other within their species. I try to make a passage in as good, safe, reasonable time as I can—that is the extent of my competitiveness.

The thought of solitude is, to me, not onerous. It would be nirvana, of course, to have someone else along perhaps, but often—most of the time—this is not possible for myriad reasons, and so I accept solitude. I have sailed with many other people; probably over a thousand of them. Most of them, if they appeared before me now, I would greet with open arms; others I would jump over the side to avoid. I can be introverted or extroverted, depending on my mood or the circumstances, but I have a need, which perhaps only sailors, writers and monks know, for inward reflection and contemplation. I know that these can only be achieved in isolation. When I am alone my perceptions are vastly heightened and the absence of other people brings my experiences to me much less diluted, more vivid, more sharply defined, and more well-remembered. For these reasons, the company of others I am willing to forego.

I suspect that my lack of fear of solitude is something of a curiosity to some people. In a few it may even arouse a certain hostility; a suspicion that, because I do not succumb to society's incessant clamor to deny my own individuality, to submerge it in a social and "cooperative" (yet essentially uncooperative) endeavor, there might be something "wrong" with me. I am certain that in my solitude I have been able to see, much more clearly, the meaning and richness of what is in the world and all around it, and in my lone contemplations I have grown in mental and spiritual stature. Besides, I consider that fear of being alone is merely a symptom of self-pity, and to me self-pity is the deadliest sin of all—the root of most of the twentieth century's problems. To me, there is no sense in feeling sorry for myself simply because some land-locked Viennese cocaine addict scribbled that I should, and so I don't. I generally consider that I exist for solutions, not for problems. When I am alone at sea I know I am sure of myself, and that I, and I alone, am in charge of my destiny. Many people never, not even for a brief five minutes in a whole lifetime, know the joy of that knowledge.

But there's yet one more motivation in exploration, certainly where the sailors and the sea are concerned, and probably the mountaineers and the mountains, and the polar explorers and the wastes of ice. I know that I have it, and always have had, yet there seems to be no name for it. It has been called "The Ulysses factor," but that sounds a bit pretentious to me. It is a drive—a power which drags me, sometimes even against my will, back to the seas. It is mysterious; so much so that it almost defies expression. It is as if the sea pulls me to her, as if she knows that a part of me belongs to her, as if she calls me, as if she knows that I taste her in my own sweat and sniff her in my nostrils and know the salt of her in my own blood, and am unable to deny her call. It is as if *my body*— not *me*, but *my body*—remembers a time when humanity belonged in the sea, and as if she, like a mother whom I have abandoned, is drawing me to her with arms strong and implacable. Yet I don't love the sea; respect is more the word.

But to most ocean voyagers, and certainly to me, the questions "who, what, when and how" almost always come before "why" when we think of the sea and her beautiful, terrible, siren-song.

Lecture given at the Explorers Club, New York, 1978

EPISODE 15

Bernard Moitessier— A Windmill Tilter

In over fifty years' wandering the world's oceans, mostly under sail in small craft, time and circumstances dictated that I would meet many remarkable and memorable people. One of the most extraordinary, and certainly one of the most memorable of the sailors I met, was Bernard Moitessier.

In many places, at many times, I have been accused of Francophobia. It's true that I have criticized French characteristics, but only of the individuals I have written or spoken of. My greatest hero is a Frenchman.

I first had the privilege to meet Bernard in Sausalito, California, in 1980. He was moored there in his steel ketch *Joshua*. Our wakes had crossed many times in the previous years, but somehow we had always seemed to miss each other in port. On our first meeting Bernard lectured me on my terrible habits, such as eating roast beef, smoking and drinking whisky. He told me I was bound to develop ulcers if I went on like that. I told him I would rather have ulcers in my stomach than in my mind; he gave up trying to convert me to asceticism. Having sounded each other out, we turned our conversation to other matters, such as how to get more youngsters into sailing, which has always been one of my hobby-horses. Bernard's English was very good, but when he was short of a word he would break into French. I think he was pleased that I understood him perfectly.

We went below in *Joshua*, ate rice and vegetables and drank fresh water—that must have been the first fresh water I drank in years. I remember that we talked about gardening, of which he seemed to know a great deal, while I knew nothing at all. Then, while Bernard silently meditated, I looked around *Joshua*'s cabin.

It was a hot, damp, untidy, sprawling space, the whole length of the vessel from the companionway forward to the bow, full of unmade beds, incense sticks smoking away, and tiny cupboards jammed with anti-ulcer pills and other remedies for stomach-ailments.

Bernard was almost the same age as I, but you couldn't find two men more different. About the only thing we had in common was our physical build—spare, our interest in literature and classical music, and our love for long-distance voyaging. He was a dreamer, a mystic, who drew people towards him, in quiet circles, while I was a catalyst for action, and reveled in activating others to strive in all directions.

I met Bernard again in California in early 1981. He didn't seem to have much money then. I recall watching him pass through a small airport lounge, wondering that no one seemed to know that in their midst was one of the world's greatest-ever ocean-voyagers. He was having problems with the U.S. immigration authorities, and figuratively wading, neck deep, in a sea of bureaucratic forms and other paper nonsense. I liked Bernard so much that, even though I was myself technically an "illegal alien" (my visa had expired by a few months), I made a public appeal from my lecture platform for someone to help him. I even wrote to one very famous America's Cup racing and media "personality" with many political contacts, appealing for his help for Bernard to stay in California; no answer was the loud reply. In December 1982, Bernard was eventually forced to sail away in *Joshua*, unprepared mentally or physically for a long sea voyage, heading for the Pacific Islands. He first made for the southern tip of Baja California in Mexico, and there he lost *Joshua* in a sudden cyclonic wind that bodily threw *Joshua* ashore.

Thanks to friends—most of them American—Bernard

was soon provided with a new boat, *Tamata*, and sailed for the
Pacific Islands in 1983.

During our meetings, Bernard told me much of his life
story. It seemed to me to be straight out of Joseph Conrad. He
was born in 1925 in Hanoi, when Vietnam was part of the
French colony of Indochina. His parents had shipped out
there from France after the First World War. His father was in
the import/export business in Saigon; his mother was a
painter of some distinction. During school holidays, Bernard
was sent to a small village near Ha Tien, on the Gulf of Thailand in South Vietnam. There, with the local fishermen, he
learned the rudiments of sailing. In 1946, the French-Vietnam
War broke out; Bernard spent the same year in military service
in a French Navy coastal craft. Then, until 1952, he sailed regularly in local fishing craft around Ha Tien, and there built his
first boat, a small junk he named *Marie-Thérèse*.

In 1952 Bernard departed from Kampot, in Cambodia, on
his first long sea-passage. He had intended to voyage to
France, by way of the Cape of Good Hope, but was wrecked
on the coral reefs of Diego Garcia Island, in the southern Indian Ocean. Navigation before the days of satellite systems
was a tenuous and risky business. Pounded on the reefs,
Marie-Thérèse was a total loss.

Penniless, with only the clothes he was wearing—not
even a pair of shoes—Bernard worked his way onboard a
passing steamer 2000 miles to the island of Mauritius (then
British but with French spoken). In Mauritius, he worked for
three years, spearfishing, charcoal-making, and as manager of
a fish-factory on the lonely atolls of Cargados Carajos, out in
the ocean northeast of Mauritius.

During the three years on Mauritius, Bernard built his
second boat, *Marie-Thérèse II*. She was another junk-style vessel, the kind he knew and understood. He sailed from Mauritius in 1956 and made for Durban, South Africa. There, to raise
money for his further voyage home to France, he worked as a

shipwright. From Durban, after a year, he made his way around the Cape of Good Hope to Cape Town, and worked in a clay pottery making cups and dishes.

In 1958, Bernard sailed for the West Indies, and in *Marie-Thérèse II* was wrecked again on the windward side of the island of St. Lucia.

Penniless again, Bernard made his way to Martinique, where he landed a working berth in an oil tanker, which, after six months tramping around the Atlantic Ocean, eventually got him to France. There he wrote his first book, *Sailing to the Reefs*. The book was an immediate success in France, and on the proceeds, in 1962, Bernard built his ketch *Joshua*. He also married Françoise, his first wife. Bear in mind this was long before the days of "push-button navigation." It was all sextant, guess, and God. The difference between ocean-voyaging then and now is probably more than between crossing America in a Conestoga wagon and in a jumbo jet.

As soon as *Joshua* was built, Bernard and Françoise headed for the Mediterranean, where, in two seasons, they earned enough money running an onboard sailing school to sail west-about via Panama for Tahiti. In those days life was simpler, but sailing was, before the electronic revolution, more complex and difficult, and a host of recently-developed materials and techniques were as yet untried and tested. Never underestimate the courage and ingenuity of the ocean-sailing pioneers in the middle of the 20th century. In comparison, they make the 19th-century prairie pioneers look like weekend trippers, and the wide horizons which they opened up made the old Western cowboys look like cab drivers.

From Tahiti, in 1966, Bernard and Françoise made one of the longest long-distance small-craft voyages up to that time: they sailed back to Europe non-stop for four months east-about around Cape Horn. In Spain, where *Joshua* had arrived, unheralded, unremarked, and almost unnoticed, Bernard wrote his second book, *Cape Horn: The Logical Route*.

His second book brought Bernard Moitessier international notice, not only as a daring voyager, but also as an erudite and fluent writer of the sea. Now his writing was known not only in France, but also in England and the U.S. (where, for some obscure and illogical reason his book was retitled *The First Voyage of Joshua*).

In 1968 the British newspaper "Observer" organized the first-ever round-the-world non-stop single-handed ocean sailing race, the Golden Globe Race, starting from Plymouth. When Bernard decided to take part, several British ocean sailors, some prominent, some unknown, were already entered : Nigel Tetley, Robin Knox-Johnston, Bill King, Donald Crowhurst . . . Some of the entrants were in traditional-design wooden boats, some in the new-fangled fiberglass, some monohulls, a couple of trimarans; and now here was *Joshua*, a steel monohull about as fit for racing multihulls as an ox for racing greyhounds; the entrants were a motley crew, no doubt about it.

The story of the 1968-69 Golden Globe Race is now legend among ocean sailors, and probably always will be. I was involved, but only as a mid-Atlantic radio relay in *Barbara* to Francis Chichester who was in Lisbon. I'll mention it only briefly here; how Bill King's trimaran broke up off the Cape of Good Hope, how Nigel Tetley's broke up in the South Atlantic, leaving Moitessier in the lead, and bringing the Great Pretender, Donald Crowhurst, second; and then how Bernard, in a magnificent gesture, unaware that his act would push Crowhurst into first place and to suicide, threw away all the glory of winning the race, all the advantages and prizes that would be his as soon as he reached Plymouth, to return to his beloved Tahiti "for his own peace of mind."

We Atlantic sailors were aware at the time that Crowhurst was pulling a fast one; for weeks, his radio signals, purporting to come from the Southern Ocean, had been traced to the South Atlantic, off Argentina. Crowhurst's demise brought a comparative unknown, Robin Knox-Johnston (now still at ocean-sailing in 1994), into the lead and to win the race. But I

have no doubt in my mind that Moitessier, when he rejected
the commercialism of the competition and turned away to follow his own course, in reality *won his own race.* For that I think
he will be remembered long after all the other competitors.
For certain he beat all records, before or since, for the most
miles covered by any single-hander without stopping: *one-
and-a-half times around the world.* To 20th-century ocean sailors,
Bernard Moitessier was what Kit Carson had been to the 19th-
century Western pioneers; yet so far as I know Carson wrote
no books, and Moitessier wrote beautifully.

For the next two years, berthed in Papeete, Tahiti, against
the waterfront (which was being made into a six-lane highway), Bernard wrote his third book, *The Long Way,* about the
Golden Globe Race. He also met and married his second wife,
Iléana. In 1972, with his wife and two-year old son, Stephan,
he sailed in *Joshua,* first for New Zealand, and then to the atoll
of Ahé, in the French Tuamotus, where they stayed for three
years, planting coconut and fruit trees and ending the plague
of rats which had been destroying the copra harvests of the is-
landers.

In 1978, Bernard and his family sailed back to Tahiti
where he wrote and grew vegetables in a small garden until
1980. But Bernard had other things on his mind besides gardening—one was the self-destructive nature of the modern
world (which the misguided call the "Western world"), pour-
ing billions of tons of noxious gases daily into the atmosphere,
and the other was the U.S.-Soviet arms race. His quixotic nature told Moitessier exactly what he should do and he did it;
or at least he tried to do it. He headed for what he imagined
was the pulsing-heart of the modern world—California—and
for three years fought a lone campaign against what he (and
practically everyone else) knew to be wrong. We quarreled,
but in a friendly way; I thought, and I still do, it was better the
world die than God and the human spirit. Besides, I told him
that human nature being what it is, communism would collapse within twenty years of its own dead weight. But during

Bernard's three years in California, besides tending a friend's vegetable garden, he wrote in longhand 606 separate, individual letters to the editors of 606 U.S. newspapers about the stupidity of the arms race, and about the need for "peace first, understanding later."

When Bernard told me later, in Paris where he was "vacationing," what he was doing, I was touched, of course, but I'm too cynical to believe that mankind will ever destroy itself, as long as it can find some other world to blow up. I advised him to either get elected in the U.S. (which was impossible), or to stop wasting his time and energy, to stop sending his book royalties to the Pope and letters to the presidents and prime ministers, and to get out of Paris as fast as he could, and go back to *Tamata* in her berth in Raiatea, near Tahiti, and teach kids to sail; it'll do him and them more good, I said. Bernard did something that windmill tilters are not supposed to usually do: he *laughed*.

Bill Tilman— A Man for All Seasons

In recent years many people have asked me: "What does it feel like to be compared with this great sailor, or that . . ." even sometimes, to what once would have been my blushes, Joshua Slocum. In reply, I usually express some kind of puzzlement and even perhaps pretend that I do not understand, and hope the question will fade.

Secretly, though, I wish to myself that it was Bill Tilman to whom I was being compared; without any doubt, Bill was the greatest adventurer-writer who has ever put pen to paper or stepped onboard a boat. He was certainly, to my mind, one of the greatest sail voyagers of this or any other age. As an explorer, his name can perhaps rank with Cook, Bougainville, Shackleton and Amundsen; as a writer, with Conrad, Gerbault, and certainly with Slocum. Anyone who knew the man and his books, and can read at all between the lines must admit that, all things considered, Bill Tilman far outranks Conrad in penetrating the depths of men's souls *in extremis*.

Francis Chichester, Bernard Moitessier, Irving Johnson, Edward Alcard, Clare Francis, Naomi James—I've known some of the most famous small-craft sailors and sailing authors of the 20th century. But of all the voyaging people I ever met in my 50 years and more of sea voyaging (when I wasn't up some remote river) in small craft, the one who strikes me as the most memorable was Bill Tilman, probably better known to readers as *W.H.Tilman*. It's a pity that Bill is so little known among modern sailors; but such seems to be the usual fate of unsponsored, self-supporting voyagers. With no big-business to boost their *fame*, with only their own wits and pen to support them, unsponsored ocean voyagers either have a thin time when they're alive or a long shelf of books to leave when they're dead. Luckily Bill Tilman left us a long shelf of books and what books they are!

Bill was the author of a dozen or so volumes describing his mountaineering and sailing adventures. His life was packed with adventure; born in 1898, he fought as a gunnery officer in the British Army in the blood-soaked battlefields of World War One, then he spent fourteen years growing coffee in East Africa. In the 1920s, he made the first-ever east-west 3000-mile bicycle trip across Africa, living mainly on bananas.

Bill Tilman became a mountaineer in the 1930s. He climbed in China, Afghanistan, and the Himalayas; he was the first to the summit of mighty Nanda Devi. Remember, this was long before the days of jet planes whisking people around the world in ease and comfort.

Then followed World War Two, with Bill again as a gunner, fighting in the Middle East, North Africa, and Italy. For a time after the war he was British Consul in Maymyo, Burma, and again took to the mountains of Sinkiang and Nepal.

Easily-reached mountains, however, were not enough for Bill. He took to sailing, to reach remote unclimbed mountains in the Arctic and Antarctic. In the process, simply as means to his ends, and never as ends in themselves, Bill Tilman made some of the most remarkable long-distance small-craft voyages of this century. The sweep of his reaches are incredible, especially considering that in those days there was no "push-button" satellite-navigation.

Bill's voyages—except his last—were made in elderly Bristol Channel Pilot cutters; gaff-rigged, top-sailed, straight-bowed, spoon-sterned, heavily rigged luggers that needed half a gale to shift them at any decent speed, but how they shifted then! Because of his heavy old boats, Bill always needed a crew, but he could rarely keep them long, and even more rarely did they ever sail with Bill for more than one passage. Bill couldn't afford professional paid hands; his crewmen usually came from the most unlikely sources: Oxford University undergraduates straight out of the classrooms, or respondents to ads in the London "Times" agony (personal) column under the headings "Sailing Trips," or "Holidays and Chalets." We may only imagine what they thought when they learned they were expected to head for the frozen wastes of the high polar seas for months at a time in a decrepit, 60-year-old, leaky, gaff-cutter with a rusty engine and patched sails, along with a studious-looking but extremely tough old man of quiet but biting comment in his 60s or 70s.

Bill was not a man to suffer fools gladly. Tilman would have taken a very dim view of the current type of "celluloid hero." With one cutting remark he would have stopped any would-be "Rambo" or "Crocodile" in his tracks. He had an uncanny, almost genetic, sense of what was "phony" and what was not, and he never hid his feelings on that. Bill was by no means the heavy, boozy, macho type at all, and he thoroughly disliked such people. It was Bill Tilman, in fact, who first indicated to me the fallacy in Ernest Hemingway's "macho-man stance." Bill was slightly built (as are most ocean voyagers) but wiry. He had Celtic blue-green eyes which seemed to penetrate me. He had about him almost the look of a very active, holidaying schoolmaster, but I remember he never spoke down at me, as his "class-sense" might have led him to, had he not been who he was.

I first met Bill in 1959, in Reykjavik, Iceland. He was then in his early 60s and I was 35. Bill was in his old gaff cutter *Mischief*; his erstwhile crewmen had seen the light, after a four-month voyage to the mountains of East Greenland, and deserted him. It was understandable. Cooking in *Mischief* was done in a metal bucket; clothes washing was only allowed at the end of a voyage. He had very good practical reasons for such matters.

As the only two foreign "yachtsmen" in town, Bill and I were invited to dinner by a certain Scandinavian ambassador to Iceland. We both donned our best shore-going rigs (such as they were). At the ambassador's residence, we were sat—me a bit self-consciously—at a white-clothed table replete with gleaming silverware. As usual at Scandinavian functions then, our hosts and fellow guests were quite stiff and formal. To set the conversational ball rolling Bill regaled us with tales from his mountain-climbing days in the Himalayas. We were all entranced. If ever there was an all-round raconteur it was Bill Tilman. Then our hostess, the (rather disdainful, I thought) ambassador's wife had Icelandic "beer" served to each guest. In those days the local beer was about as strong as tap water. Bill hesitated for a moment or two in some marvelous account of the vertical ascent of some remote Nepalese crag on the roof of the world, to pour his beer into his glass, and take a sip. I sipped mine—it was like dishwater. The looks on my mug and Bill's ascetic face as we both stared at each other over the table—the slightest rise of one of his shaggy eyebrows, me trying to not show my distaste for those soapsuds—must have spoken volumes. Only to us, though; we said nothing. The rest of the meal, until the last course, passed in complete silence from Bill, while our Scandinavians stumblingly maintained a halting conversation in English (their English was a kindness for us). For the last of five courses, the ambassador's rather snooty wife served us yogurt in elegant but tiny blue-and-white china pots, each about the size of an egg cup. Silently, dutifully, Bill scraped his tiny spoonful of yogurt out of his little pot. A skull's grimace, he had.

The ambassador's wife beamed a glowing smile at Bill. "Jou see, Meester Teelman," she exclaimed, "I haff served jogurt here especially for jou to remind jou off jour beee-autiful mountains in Nepal," she shouted down the table for the benefit of all present.

Bill's death's-head mournfully peered over his rimless half-spectacles at our hostess for a couple of seconds, while silence settled on the dinner party. Bill intoned in his cultured "terribly English" voice slowly, low, and cutting : "Madam," he said, measuredly, "Madam, in Nepal . . . yogurt is served in *full-sized chamber pots!*"

I spent the rest of the evening trying desperately not to splutter with mirth while all our fellow hosts sat silently, their faces beet-red, until it was time for Bill and me to take our leave. I honestly never thought that Bill had been intentionally rude; he was not accustomed to the company of women, and simply did not know how to deal with them. He never had a woman in his crew, despite his frequent plaints about the lack of the "feminine touch" in his craft. Various theories were bandied about the cruising and exploration circles; most of them were expounded by people who never knew Bill, and most of them were, I am sure, dead wrong. Bill's reputed "misogyny" (if such it was) is explained by the fact that most of the women in the British upper-middle-class circles in which he was brought up were by today's western standards, except for a very few exceptions, spoiled and "wimpy." This might, or might not, have been their own fault—that's a question for more knowledgeable people than I to decide. It had been different in my own "working class." My mother sailed regularly with my father. In Bill's "class," women had not been willing, as many modern western women are, to "rough it" with their men-folk, and even fewer to do it alone. It was "simply not done by ladies." In those days, under sail, on long voyages, especially in polar regions, "roughing it" hardly expresses the endless, comfortless misery.

The way Bill Tilman roughed it—always on a shoestring—very few other men of his social class were willing to share life onboard with him, either. Even I would have thought twice about it. I lived rough, but I was easy with others. Bill was not, by any means, an easy skipper. For women, Bill was born fifty years too early; for men one hundred years too late. He was, perhaps like all great men, a living anachronistic paradox. I suppose that to understand Bill Tilman thoroughly one would have to be the master of practically every art and science known—and a few others besides.

The next time I encountered Bill and *Mischief* was in 1961. She was at anchor in a lonely fjord near Godthåb, in southwest Greenland. I sighted her as the legendary dying Foreign Legionnaire is supposed to sight the mirage of a cool oasis. I had spoken with no-one except my dog for weeks on a very hard trip from Svalbard. Here was, I imagined, again, at last, the warmth of human company—and English-speaking, too! Excitedly anticipating, I worked my own boat *Cresswell* in up the windless fjord (my engine, as usual, was on strike), to tie up alongside the massive pine sides of *Mischief* and make fast.

"Ahoy, *Mischief!*" I crowed, my voice crackling in the cold. No reply; only the plaintive cries of seabirds as they wheeled over *Cresswell's* stern in futile hope of food. (There were so few cruising yachts in those days that the seabirds would foolishly imagine we were fishermen; nowadays they know better.) I busily bundled myself over the high bulwarks of *Mischief* and made my way aft to her main companionway. Again I sang out, "Anyone aboard?" Again there was silence but for the steady squeak of rudder pintles.

I excitedly and noisily clattered down the companionway steps to Bill's main cabin. I was imagining all kinds of fond welcomes and hearty pats on my back. I hadn't seen *Mischief* for over two years; I hadn't spoken with anyone except my dog Nelson for weeks. Apart from the dim light of a tiny oil lamp and the glimmer of Bill's steel-rimmed glasses at the far end of a plain scrubbed wooden table, together with the reddish glow from a coal-burning stove on the amidships, all was darkness. I stood for a second or two to become accustomed to the dimness. I saw that Bill was sitting darning a sock.

Then Bill's voice, quiet, cultured, calm, penetrating, came at me through the gloom, "Oh, it's Llangareth, is it?"(That's

the name of my own bit of the Principality of Wales, you see).
Bill spoke as if I were one of his crew and he had seen me daily
for months.

I was too astonished to reply. I stood like a fool for a few
seconds. It was like being sluiced with icy Arctic water, but at
least he'd remembered the matter of Llangareth. He went on,
"I suppose you want a cup of tea?"

I recovered my voice, "It's me, Bill . . . "

"I can see that," he said. "Well, you know where the stove
is . . . you can put the kettle on. I'm busy now, but later, when
you've made the tea, I'll join you, if you don't mind!"

That was Bill's way of welcome. It never made sense to
me, until I reached my own 60s. Now it makes all the sense in
the world. In the Arctic, why waste time and energy on useless exclamations of welcome when the offer of a warm drink
is far more important? Why express excitement or surprise
that we had survived to encounter one another again? Would
it not perhaps lead us to wonder if we were capable of sur-
vival? Should it not be treated as the most normal, every day
occurrence? Of course Bill was right. Dead right.

Bill went out of this life in the mid-1970s; still one of the
world's innocents—I'm convinced of that. When he was mod-
est about his knowledge of maritime things he was not pretending. It wasn't that he was ignorant, for all his long
voyages, about the sea or the ways of the sea; it was simply
that his mind and heart were always in the far, unreachable
mountains. Why else would he have departed from Rio de
Janeiro in an old harbor tugboat "converted to sail"—some
leaky old tub in which you and I would not cross a duck-
pond—but to reach and conquer the otherwise unreachable,
wind-blasted mountains of South Georgia Islands of the
Southern Ocean? I like to think that St. Peter duplicated on the
far reaches of Heaven's ocean the mountains of South Georgia
specially for Bill to voyage to and to climb, and that the angels
perhaps provided a large chamber pot full of yogurt for him
to do it on! To anyone looking for vicarious splendor and ex-

citement you can do no better than look for a book with the name *Mischief* in the title, or by "H.W. Tilman." In the 20th century, he was the greatest of us all. I'm proud to be, like him, a son of Wales.

Clare Francis— Sailing's First Lady

In over fifty years of world-wide seafaring, mostly in small craft, life, time, and circumstances dictated that I should meet a few remarkable and memorable women. It is only in the last two decades that women have been involved in any significant numbers in ocean sailing. Before that, they were rare indeed aboard long-distance-voyaging craft; most of the women we men-sailors met were ashore, either in bars or in church, depending on our proclivities. Then in the sixties came the electronic, technical, and materials revolution that made small-craft voyaging much less hard muscle-work, so enabling couples or even women alone to handle boats in all weathers.

The women who then came into the ocean-sailing scene were, in the main, a remarkable and memorable crew, and of these one of the most remarkable and certainly memorable women I have met is, without any doubt, Clare Francis.

I first saw Clare in Newport, Rhode Island, in 1976. She had taken part in the OSTAR single-handed trans-Atlantic race, and been the first woman to finish in 29 days. On the deck of her 38-foot sloop, *Robertson's Golly*, tied up alongside the dock, she was surrounded by a bustling flotilla of male admirers, from high-power PR-vultures to scruffy boat bums. She, sun-burned and wind-blown, squinting her big blue eyes against the sun, was exchanging light banter with them all. I think we may have exchanged a few words, but I'm not sure.

I was with a woman-friend, a New Yorker, who was not interested in sailing boats, and only anxious to tour the rich peoples' mansions of Newport. By the time I had gently ditched her, and hurriedly run (I had two legs then) to where *Robertson's Golly* was berthed, there was no sign of Clare, and I had to sail for St. Thomas on the tide.

The next time I saw Clare Francis, in 1982, was in a very different place and much-changed circumstances: in a BBC (British Broadcasting Corporation) studio in London. She was the interviewer for the program—charming, gracious, patient and kind; I was by then a much-published author, publicizing my latest book. How refreshing it was, how helpful, what a delightful change for me, to be interviewed by someone—and a woman at that—who knew about sailing and voyaging! Most of the "anchorpersons" who talked to me on over 100 TV shows had less idea of what ocean-voyaging is all about than . . . the . . . the . . . person-in-the-moon, and wouldn't know an anchor from a tennis racket.

The next time I met Clare was again in London, in 1984. I had sailed there from San Diego in the trimaran *Outward Leg*. In Columbia, my rubber dinghy had been stolen. I needed a replacement badly for work on our forthcoming Rhine-Danube crossing of Europe. Short of funds and desperate for a dinghy I phoned Clare. This will show you how she is: she turned up right away through London's busy traffic, at St. Katherine's Dock. "What do you need, Tristan?" she asked me, all smiles.

"A 12-foot dinghy," I replied.

"It'll be with you in the morning," she told me. "I can't stay . . . I'm in the middle of a new book . . . "

At the time, although I would have loved to chat with Clare, that suited me fine; I was in the middle of my own book, *Outward Leg* (*A Star to Steer Her By* in the U.K.), but that's how I got the very last rubber dinghy made by the Dunlop Company of Liverpool, donated by them, courtesy of Clare Francis.

When Clare was born is irrelevant; she's one of those women who will always be young at heart, and anyway, no gentleman would dream of mentioning a lady's age. She was born at Thames Ditton, in the English countryside west of London. Her father is a retired senior civil-servant (in fact he was, among other things, responsible for re-lighting London after the depredations of six war years). Clare's mother was described in PR handouts as a "housewife," I found her to be a most literate, informed, wise and charming woman. Every summer during Clare's childhood, the family moved to a house by the sea, and there she, from the age of seven, crewed in her father's sailing dinghy. By her early teens, Clare was the local dinghy champion. At eleven, she took up ballet lessons, and was accepted, after a time, by the Royal Ballet School. There she underwent a rigorous, and for her miserable, five-year, strenuous existence in an ambiance of cutthroat competition. At 17, she decided she was not made for ballet, and concentrated on the studying of economics at the University of London. Then followed five years in marketing, and as a food production manager, with Clare always dreaming of "a new direction" to her life.

Clare is of the Generation-That-Would-Not-Wait. When she was in her mid-twenties she, her then man-friend, and a few kindred-spirits decided to pool their resources together to build an ocean yacht and sail round the world, "earning their way as they went." It is one of the oldest dreams on earth; it is also one of the most failed. The number of people—especially young people—who have done it can be counted in tens. As certain in resolution as a Greek tragedy, as the realities of the "dream" became apparent, the kindred spirits took off at disparate tangents; then Clare's man-friend dropped out, leaving only her to hold the dream and bring it to her own form of reality. Seven months later, having borrowed and begged the means, she had acquired the 32-foot cruiser *Gulliver G*, eight weeks' food, a good book on celestial navigation, a copy of Tolstoy's *War and Peace*, and plenty of classical music (opera mostly) tapes. With those, she departed England on her first trans-Atlantic voyage, to Newport, Rhode Island, by way of the Azores.

Asked how she dealt with her emotions on her first off-shore voyage, Clare's brief reply shows more about her character than anything else. "I frightened myself fairly thoroughly, but 20 years' experience in small boats saw me through," she said.

Clare didn't say "I was scared," or "The seas frightened me," or "I was terrified of the storms, the dark, of being all alone out there . . ." No, she said she "frightened herself." That's a real ocean-sailor talking.

Having reached Newport, Clare wrote a few magazine articles and then set off slowly heading south to the Caribbean. Then something happened which should be re-membered by all women, because it marked a turning-point in their acceptance as capable sailors. En route to the Caribbean, Clare met Eve Bonham, another British woman, who persuaded her to join her in the Round-Britain Race the next spring. Theirs would be the first-ever all-women's crew in that or any other major ocean race. A sponsor was quickly found and the women finished a very tough race through rough sea areas—third out of a field of 65 starters. From then on, there would be no turning back for women sailors; no more, unless they acquiesced, relegation to the galley; no more, unless they enjoyed or tolerated it, being shouted at by unsure-of-anything men-skippers; no more, unless they pre-ferred it, being left at home on sailing opportunities.

Once Clare had tasted sail-racing, there was no stopping her for several years: The British-Azores Race in 1975 (tenth out of 60 starters), the OSTAR trans-Atlantic solo race in 1976 (which was filmed on BBC camera), and in 1978 she was the first woman-skipper on the Whitbread Round-the-World race (fifth out of 15 starters).

Clare had by now a son, Tom (first kid up the masthead on *Outward Leg*) and three sailing books published, *Come*

Hell or High Water (1976), *Come Wind or Weather* (1978), and *The Commanding Sea* (1981). But she, like many other sailing authors before her, realized that, after the first glows of novelty die to a shivering shimmer, the task of writing non-fiction accounts about sail voyages is far more difficult and onerous than staying the course in any other kind of race. Very, very few (I can think of only one) non-fiction sailing authors have managed to hold any wide public interest for more than one or two books. Besides, in my own experience, writing fiction is easier by far than writing of factual events; the author can allow imagination free range, and there is little of the drudge of research and absolute accuracy of facts. But her ocean-passages, and the three books she wrote about her own experiences in them, were for Clare merely a road, conscious or not, toward what she really wanted to do: write fiction.

In 1982, Clare's chance came. Her London publisher asked her to write another book about sailing. Clare was on holiday in the Scilly Islands, southwest of England. She poked around in the cottage she was renting and found some old diaries from World War Two. She thought they held the plot of a good war novel, proposed it to her agent, who auctioned it with nine publishers, and was rewarded with the highest advance ever paid in Britain for a first novel. This was *Night Sky*, which in 1983 established Clare Francis in 22 countries as an acclaimed author of good fiction. This first novel was on the "New York Times" bestseller list for ten weeks. Two more novels in Clare's favorite theme—the "spy-thriller"—have followed: *Red Crystal*, in 1985, and *Wolf Winter*, in 1987.

But for all the success in fiction-writing and publishing, one historical fact remains: in 1974 Clare Francis and Eve Bonham lit an inextinguishable navigation-lamp for women worldwide. Whatever Clare, with her justified literary ambitions, thinks of her present and future persona as a fiction author, and not a special kind of sailor, nothing can change the incontrovertible fact that she was one of three women (the

odd one out is Naomi James) who for all time, must be ac-
knowledged as being in the first rank of ocean sailors. No library shelf, no matter how long, no matter how crammed
with best-seller fiction, can, or will, ever change that fact.

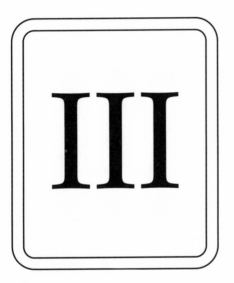

EPISODE 18

Lost Opportunities

I doubt if many young people (or older, come to that) realize how so much of the coastlines of the world's landmasses have changed over the past forty years.

Back in the '50s and early '60s, a long-distance sail voyager was bound to call in on islands or coasts which until then had not been changed at all, or, as the lie nowadays is, "developed." These were the days before faster, efficient, safe mass travel was made possible by the introduction of large passenger-jets. Before that, travel had mostly been ashore by train, and at sea by ship. It took at least five days to cross the Atlantic Ocean by ocean liner, but more often much longer. It would have taken about ten days, by the old propeller airplane routes, to fly from London to Bangkok, and about six weeks by sea via the Suez Canal.

You could say that in those days most of the world's coasts, with the exceptions of some new shipping ports, Biarritz, the French Riviera, some tiny bits of the Baltic and Italy, stretches of beach in Florida and California and around Sydney and Rio, plus a few invasion beaches here and there, were exactly as they had been at the turn of the century. Even the holiday resorts in the British Isles would have been quite familiar to any mid-Victorian time traveler. Much of the coastlines of what is now called the "developing world," apart from a fishing village here and there, were still exactly as they must have been when our ancestors abandoned the sea to breed ashore millions of years ago.

It's only in looking back that I reflect how "innocent" we were in those days. We weren't really—human nature doesn't change much over the course of a generation or two—but time and change certainly make us seem to have been so. For instance, in 1954, my sloop *Banjo* was reputedly the first foreign yacht (long-distance sailing yachts were then rare indeed) to call in at any Spanish port since before the Spanish Civil War had begun, back in 1936. The port was Ibiza in the western Mediterranean, and it came about because I had been becalmed for over two weeks, and was running out of fresh water. Blue skies might be dreams come true for a vacationer, but for a small-craft sailor with less than an inch of drinking water left in his tank, they can be a nightmare.

To cut a long story sideways, I made my way into Ibiza Harbor. Talk about another world. In Ibiza Town, the clock had not merely stopped in 1936, it had actually been put back another fifty years, too, by (apart from other things) apathy, punitive labor laws for the workers who remained alive, and rigid police control. Apart from a steamship (real, hissing, clanking, steam) in the old cobblestone port, a rusty, wheezing bus, and a couple of open cars from the 1920s, there was simply no sign of the 20th century in Ibiza. The town, both inside and outside the old walls, was full of older women dressed in black garments which reached to their boots. I learned that these were the widows of Republican government supporters who had been killed or executed by dictator Franco's firing squads, or been flung from the high cliffs about the old town, during and after the Civil War. Except for one or two, the males in town were glowering, strutting party police, shoddily dressed, dirty soldiers, or either very, very young or very, very old.

Ibiza in '54 was one of the two inhabited places I was ever in (apart from London's Holloway women's prison on a brief visit in 1968) where there were no civilian men of breeding age. The only other place had been during World War Two, at

Hawick, on the Scotland/England border, where the armed forces uniform textile spinning mills had been located supposedly out of reach of Nazi long-distance bombers (that's another tale), but that situation didn't last long once the Navy sailors got word of it, you can bet your life; some idiot blurted, Jolly Jack was hot on the trail of "a bit of the other," and in three days the place had been so full of sailors it was more like Portsmouth barracks.

Anyway, back to my opportunities tale: in Ibiza Town, in a small fisherman's bar in the port, I first met the young son of an Army major who had been rewarded by Franco with a huge grant of land which had formerly belonged to Republican farmers and peasants. His son was a quiet rebel, being (of necessity, in secret) democratically inclined. I'll call him Eduardo. We struck up a friendship and he took me, in his pony and trap, sightseeing around the then-village of Santa Eulalia. It was there, on the beach, that Eduardo offered to sell me, on behalf of his father, (who had been driven up in a 1929 Lagonda, and was nodding vigorously in agreement) most of the eastern half of Ibiza Island for the sum of *one thousand American dollars*. I turned down Eduardo's offer because, apart from my boat, I had only fifty dollars to my name. Besides, what would I do with *land*? I was spending most of my time and energies in sailing craft, avoiding it. I was so salt-water-fond that the mere sight of soil put me off, and the (then to me) sinister sound of the surf on a beach was enough to give me the creeps; the noise of breakers on rocks used to sicken me.

Around the Mediterranean Sea in the 50s and 60s, other such memorably cheap offers of land, while not an everyday thing, were not rare. In 1963, I was offered land on the island of Formentera for as little as one cent U.S. a square meter. Now, in 1994, covered with villas, a sunny space in the European Union, with electricity, water, and gas laid on, and pensions down the road at the Post Office, it's worth a king's ransom.

In South Turkey in 1970, for one thousand dollars (a mystically magic figure it seemed then) I was offered a steep hill topped by a Crusader castle right slap bang on what was later to become one of the Eastern Mediterranean's busiest vacation area, Antalya. The Crusader castle was, it was said by the seller, part of the deal. The castle had enough room for a regiment, but it was mostly in ruins, and there was no roof. Still, a bit of hard work and ingenuity would have fixed that. But I was broke . . . and again, what would I do with stones and rocks and soil? Much later, I called at Antalya again and found that the whole thing—hill and castle—had been turned by the government into a National Park, so maybe I didn't lose out so much after all.

The most memorable offer of real estate I ever had was on the island of Gomera, the southernmost of the Canary Islands. It was in 1964, and it wasn't land, but a small house. I was exploring round the small but busy waterfront of the capital town of the island, in the cool of the evening, and stopped to admire a row of fisher folk's houses. They were obviously very old, and although they were all different, they made a long, very picturesque, terrace. One house in particular caught my eye; it had a huge, flower-bedecked window box that overhung the town quay by a meter and more. It was like something in a medieval picture. I could imagine some romantically-inclined troubadour (how the devil did they hide their inclinations in those tight breeches?) in the street below, where I stood, serenading a lady sitting in the window box above (probably while her jealous husband or lover silently prepared a chamber-pot for chucking out onto the minstrel).

As I gazed at the fine carving and trellis-work on the window box, an old gentleman in a black suit and beret came up and introduced himself, in the polite Spanish way, as the owner of the house. He was far too polite to ask me right away, but eventually it came out: was I interested in buying it?

I asked the old man how much, half expecting the reply he gave me: "Mil dólares americanos, por favor," *one thousand American dollars*. I made my excuses and we parted, for I had to leave next morning for Barbados on a trans-Atlantic ocean delivery of a 42-foot ketch which awaited me in the port.

It was only several years after, on another call in Gomera, that I discovered that the house with the overhanging window box had been none other than the last lodging of Christopher Colombus in 1492 AD, the night before he had departed from the island of Gomera onboard his caravel *Santa Maria* to "discover America," and it had, it was said, *been demolished to make way for a gasoline station*.

Many and many a time since, in my more mercenary moments, I have reflected what a fortune I could have made by simply taking apart carefully that old house, and re-erecting it in say Miami, or New York, or You-name-it in the U.S. The door money (for the amount of dollar lay-out) would have perhaps made even Disney World's receipts look paltry.

But then again, I always cheer myself by reflecting that if I'd ever made money as easily as that I wouldn't have had to continue sailing and writing, and what's anyone's life worth if you don't do what you're created to do?

Lost Loves

No matter how many craft a person has sailed during his time messing about in boats, there has to be one or two, or perhaps a few, that he or she remembers with special fondness. Some of the boats I've sailed in over the past fifty years, and that I recall the most fondly, would hardly pass muster at any decent marina nowadays; many others were first-class, state-of-the-art-at-that-time ocean greyhounds, and most of those I hardly ever give thought to. Hindsight, and especially hard times remembered, I suppose, lend a kind of charm or grace to even the crankiest old lugger.

Most people nowadays, it seems, start in small boats and work their way up to bigger ones over the years. I did the reverse. The first sailboat I lived in was a sea-going "boomie-ketch"—a "Dandy" as they were called—a cargo barge named *Second Apprentice* (described in *A Steady Trade*). That was in England, in 1938; she'd been built sixty years before, in 1878. She was 98 feet long, about 20 feet beam, and her bowsprit reached forward another 20 feet. She was constructed of pine on oak frames; her sides were a foot thick. Her main mast was about 90 feet high; her topmast loomed up another 20 feet above that. Her cross section was almost square, so she could sit on any beach for loading and discharging cargo. She may have looked cumbrous, but my, did she sail! With a crew of only two men and two boys, she could beat against wind and a five-knot river current and still make four knots over the ground. On her sides, she had massive iron leeboards, 18 feet long and eight feet broad at the fan, to help her go to windward. Her anchor weighed two tons and was brought up with a windlass that was pushed by two boys traipsing round and round.

The cargoes we carried were not at all romantic—empty mineral water bottles and scrap-iron to Germany, cheese from Holland, house bricks to the British Channel Islands, and cattle-offal back—but no quinquereme of Nineveh's crew ever sailed with more intense pride than did we lads of the "Dandys." *Second Apprentice* was sunk in the North Sea by a Nazi bomb in 1941 . . .

My next love was a very different boat indeed. *Cresswell* (*Ice!*) had been built in London in 1908 for the British Royal National Lifeboat Institution, a voluntary sea rescue service, as a beach-launched, sailing rescue boat to reach ships in distress and save lives. She was 36 feet long and seven feet at her broadest. Her length overall was deceiving. Six feet at each end of her hull, she was so sharply-pointed that her ideal crewman would have had to be a midget acrobat with one leg. For all intents and purposes of any adult human movement, she was only 24 feet long. She was built of Burmese mahogany—double-diagonal, two inches thick—on Portuguese grown oak frames. She was the best-built boat of any kind that I ever saw, and about the worst-designed boat for use as a "yacht." She was fitted together like a Rolls-Royce motor car. She positively hummed with strength. Her draft was only two feet six inches full loaded with stores for a year, so for purists that puts her into the category of a "small craft." She had twin oak bilge-keels. These I replaced with galvanized iron, and fitted a ton and a half of kentledge (cut lead) in her bilge as ballast. I replaced her old short, stubby mast with a hollow pine Norwegian main and a solid mizzen, gave her a bowsprit, called her a ketch, and sailed her farther north in the Arctic than any other private vessel had ever ventured. It cost me just over one thousand U.S. dollars to buy and refit her.

Nowadays, when I look back on some of my escapades in *Cresswell*, I wonder how I ever managed to survive. It was like sailing a gravy-dish, with all that sail up and no deep-keel. She was blown over and dismasted six times while I was in her. The last I heard of *Cresswell* was in the late '70s. She was still in commission, in Arenys de Mar, Spain, being used by an English film actress as a floating dog kennel for her pets so as to avoid British quarantine laws when she returned home.

Banjo (*Saga of a Wayward Sailor*) was the sailboat I loved the most of all. She was 25 feet LOA. She was the most kind, considerate, the most forgiving, and certainly the sweetest sailer of them all. She was so sweet and easy I could paddle her forward in a calm at a knot-and-a-half with her rudder only, by wiggling her helm back and forth. She could steer herself as if she had taken courses at it in some sailing school. A Folkboat sloop of Norwegian design, she was built of Sumatran teak on oak frames. Her deep keel of lead gave her a stability that we don't find much these days in boats twice her length. She used to grip head seas like a terrier gnarling a doglead, and in a high wind, three-reefs in, she would *worry* the living daylights out any seas, so that they had to give way to her. I never knew a boat in which I felt myself more a part of the sea as I did in *Banjo*. She was a fighter, that one! What a lovely shape she was! Her build, her sail plan, her gear, her accommodation and everything about her was the essence of simplicity.

Mind you, there's usually at least one fly in the ointment where just about every boat is concerned; *Banjo*'s main drawback was lack of headroom. Her cabin was only 5'3" high, and I was 5'11" tall. That made for an aching back and misery after a few days onboard. But she was one of those boats that always seemed to know when I was returning to her, down the jetty; always seemed to be waiting for me, quietly rejoicing at my return. Her silent anticipation was an almost inexpressible thing, but to me it was always perfectly obvious. She used to *sing* me to sleep, I loved her so.

Perhaps another reason, besides her sweetness, that I loved *Banjo* more than the other sailing craft was because she was the only boat I ever owned that was lost through someone else's ignorance and stupidity. This incompetent escaped my wrath at the time, by fleeing the scene, but God, his ears must burn every time I remember the end of *Banjo*. After dire warning, this clumsy, clutter-brained, fumble-fingered oaf anchored her at night on an open coast with no watch awake, in the Western Mediterranean. I never knew that it was possible to be so unforgiving for so long a time . . . twenty years . . . I swear it took me well over a year before I could sleep soundly in any other boat after I lost my *Banjo*. Even then, for years, I would wake in the middle of my doze, realize I was not in *Banjo*, and feel again my sense of loss. It sometimes still happens, even now.

My next love was *Sea Dart (The Incredible Voyage)*. She was originally a "Debutante" class sloop, 20 feet long, seven feet beam, bilge keeled, but specially constructed in England very strongly, of one-inch marine ply, cold molded, to make an attempt at the Northwest Passage. I suppose the man she was built for must have realized that Roald Amundsen, the Norwegian explorer, had already sailed the Northwest Passage at the turn of the century. At any rate, this plan was changed and *Sea Dart* headed across the Atlantic instead, so that I found her in Bequia, in the West Indies. With her tiny cabin and cockpit, she was too small for really serious long-voyaging; but for my purpose—to beat thousands of miles against the Humboldt Current off western South America, and then to haul her across the Andes to Lake Titicaca—she was ideal, once I'd fitted her out as a cutter so as to grab headwind better. She was a feisty little devil if there ever was one; she was as tough as nails, she could sail on wet grass; she ate and spat the wind as voraciously as she did the souls of the men who sailed in her, and she sailed, left to herself, wind-vane steered, like an angel.

The last I heard of *Sea Dart* was some years ago, she was in the Seattle, Washington, area. I had donated her for preservation in commission on condition that she be used to benefit orphaned children, but I don't yet know how this scheme has progressed, though I hope to find out when I next return to the northwest U.S.

My latest love is completely different again from all the others. She is a double-ended longtail, a motor-propelled open fishing boat, *Henry Wagner (To Venture Further)*. She is 40 feet long and seven feet beam, and draws only six inches. Despite her length, no one who might spend a night or two in her would say she was not a "small craft." She was built twenty years ago for fishing off the Similan Islands, in the Andaman Sea. She is constructed of a very hard wood, similar to iroko, on frames of the same timber. She cost fifteen hundred U.S. dollars to buy the bare hull and fit it out for sea and river exploration. I am voyaging with her through the waters of Southeast Asia, reaching and teaching severely disabled kids—salvaging them from outright beggary—to earn their own way in boats of similar build, maintaining boats and their gear, and fishing. With a crew of severely disabled kids, I voyaged one thousand miles through Thailand, and then tried to persuade the Laotian government to permit me to set off into the mighty Mekong River, to reach the kids of Laos, Cambodia, and Vietnam. The Laotians refused for reasons of their own, which they did not divulge to me.

I loved all the boats I've written about here, but none of them was more important to me than *Henry Wagner*. She is undecked, open to the intense heat and humidity, the rain and insects, the snakes and other dangers of Indochina. Her only facility of any kind are two wooden boxes amidships which can be locked. In one we kept our food and eating utensils, and in the other I kept my radio and writing materials. Other than that there is a rain- and sun-shade awning and two buckets. In contrast to *Henry Wagner*, all the aforementioned boats—even *Cresswell*—were floating palaces fit for emperors. But in none of those other boats did I ever have the same feelings of accomplishment or self-fulfillment as I had in *Henry Wagner*. In none of them did I ever feel that my life, and all the experiences, hard or easy, that I had gained, were justified by my present activity. In none of them were so many—mainly young—people's lives so changed utterly for the better. In none of them was hope so freely dispensed, nor love and respect so freely given and earned.

So what is it in our boats that we love? Surely it can't be the boat itself, a mere collection of bits and pieces put together anonymously by workmen in some far away factory or yard. Is it perhaps the spirit, some transference perhaps into the very fabric of the vessel—of the ideals, the hopes, the dreams, of the people who design and build the boats, or who have previously voyaged in them? Is this spirit then transferred in turn to us, by some process of osmosis? Is it this that we really love when we say we love a boat?

Old Dolls, Up and Dancing

I never can forget that I started my working life sailing in a "boomie-ketch," a working-cargo vessel, and I suppose I'm one of the last to have earned my living helping full-time to carry cargo under sail. Certainly I feel a far greater affinity to the trading sail ships of old than I do to the modern, maxi ocean-racers. I always feel far more at home in a dockyard than in a yacht marina or yacht club, even though some of both have been indeed hospitable to me. This is not "reverse snobbism;" it is because my origins, my roots, are deep and firm in working sail and with working sailors whom, as a boy, I learned to admire, and even, much later, to love, when I became more fully aware of my privilege of having known them, for a finer body of men never, surely, existed.

Back in the '50s and early '60s, when I was sailing small craft often in Northern European waters, there simply were no yacht marinas. Nor apart from North America, have there been any, until very recently, in other areas. Even as the parking meter for motor cars was looked upon then as a peculiarly trans-Atlantic kind of highway holdup, so the idea of a sort of parking lot for sailing- or motor-yachts was too outlandish for the few North European sailors there were. If we did not belong to a local yacht club, we anchored in river mouths or sea inlets, or behind islands, or made for existing fishing havens. In Northern Europe, many of the latter were tidal, and there were often accidents, sometimes quite serious, involving deep-keeled yachts leaning the wrong way and suddenly falling right over with a violent crash when the tide ebbed. Fishing ports were certainly noisy at night and in the early morning, and they were not clean, either.

In the '50s and '60s, now and again I would moor or anchor near to an old-time sailing- or steam-craft rotting or rusting away. They show up in the most unlikely places. A rich viewing-ground for wrecks is the west coast of South America. The Sudanese and Eritrean coast of the Red Sea, too, is a vast ships' graveyard. So is the Cape of Good Hope. There are one or two old Cape-Horner sailing ships, still whole, beached on isolated islands, such as the Falkands or South Georgia. Even now, as you read my words, the barque *Bayard*, built in Liverpool in 1864, all 220 feet of her, rests ashore, masts still standing, amid the ice and snow of Ocean Harbour, South Georgia. *Bayard* might be seen by half a dozen humans in any year; for the rest it's penguins, seabirds, and the odd wandering albatross or two. Right until the early '60s, most Spanish and Portuguese ports had a couple or more sailing ships still working, mostly in the Mediterranean fruit trade. On the east coast of South America there are rusting hulks from Punta Arenas to Manaus, a thousand miles up the River Amazon.

In Punta Arenas itself there were and still are three of the most interesting hulks: *Falstaff*, built in 1875 at Barrow, England; *Hipparchus*, one of the first sail-carrying steamers, built in 1867 in Newcastle, England; and the ex *County of Peebles*, built in 1875 in Glasgow, Scotland. All these three, linked together by a below-decks gangway, now form the breakwater to the Chilean Naval Base at Punta Arenas. They are all three tough old buggers, with only a few flakes of metal rusted off here and there. They will probably still be there in 2194 AD. One of my fondest memories is how, many years ago, I sojourned with an illicit lover for three days in the deckhouse of *Hipparchus* without being sighted by the Chilean Navy. Well, love is love, even when you're half-frozen, and at a permanent angle of 25 degrees from the horizontal.

In the 1950s, there were many old sailing ships, some still working, in North African ports and in Greece and Turkey. Australia and New Zealand have a good share of both hulks and restored sailing-craft, too. Our knowledge of those scattered old hulks, shared with a few locals, we ocean sailors kept among ourselves, as secret prizes. I recall how often I would try to clamber onboard remote, abandoned relics and look around, and imagine being onboard in their heyday. I would sometimes seem to hear, echoing around the rotting hull, a chorus from a rousing chanty, or Liverpool voices cursing and howling over the icy wind. But tough as they are, all these old wrecks, then, seemed destined to eventually disintegrate. We knew that most of them, although by no means all, had been built in the 19th century, and that many had been square-riggers, but only the more erudite among us bothered to find out their true history.

Now, over the past three decades, that's all changed. Over the years a few, a very few, dedicated people worked every spare minute they had to raise interest in ancient wrecks that have now been restored, often with most of the actual manual work being done by unpaid volunteers. These people were considered by many to be little better than cranks, going on and on about a maritime past and heritage that very few others cared about. Now more and more maritime museums are being set up all around the world, and old ships are being salvaged, towed thousands of miles, preserved, refurbished, and in many cases even restored to full working order. Crowds of paying visitors, mostly non-sailors it seems, pass daily through these places and onboard the ships. It must strike them that what they are seeing, and touching, and walking through, is not, as in Disneyland, for example, a commercial structuring of someone's imagination, but an actual working human artifact. Each one of these incredibly well-built and intricate mechanisms was once, and in many cases still is, part of someone's everyday working life. In an amusement park such as Disneyland, the average adult customer can hardly seriously imagine himself as part of any displayed scenario, whatever it is. Onboard an old sailing craft, well preserved, it is quite easy for anyone, of any age, race, creed, or sex, to reflect that he or she could very well have hewn that plank, set that rivet, hauled on that line, cooked on that stove, or slept in that berth.

We should ask ourselves why those old sailing ships are such crowd attractions. Surely it's because people see them, consciously or not, as real works of art—sculptures—that actually moved with the wind and worked for their living. Sculptures carved and put together not by professional artists with immortality in mind, but by ordinary working folk, laboring together, yet strictly hierarchically, to make something that was not only beautiful, but eminently practical, efficient, clean and very useful. In fact, a moment's reflection will show that a great part of our modern world was *made by these sailing ships*. Neither New York nor Hong Kong, neither Cape Town nor Sydney, for example, would be where they are if it were not for the fact that they were comparatively deep and safe ports-of-call for sailing ships. I'll even go so far as to say that several countries, including Mauritius, Australia, New Zealand, Chile, and Brazil, are, in their modern forms, the direct and deliberate offspring of sailing ships; the states of California, Oregon, and Washington, as well as British Columbia, certainly are.

In 1984, in St. Katherine's Dock, in London, where I had been given a free berth for my trimaran *Outward Leg*, I used to watch tourists coming and going off old Thames sailing barges with wonder on their faces. I never imagined for a minute it was wonder at the economics of moving 300 tons of cargo quietly and efficiently, with no damage to the environment, for a few pennies a mile. Those faces were surely alight with wonder that a thing of such essential utility could be built so massively, so well, so fittingly, by mere uneducated artisans.

Victorian buildings anywhere have a grandeur about them that is undeniable, however gross might be their design. But Victorian *ships* . . . Anyone who believes that our 19th century forebears were ignorant or crude should stop and stare at any of their surviving maritime works, and tremble. We shall hardly see the likes of those works made again by hands and shoulders and the sweat of human brows. We shall hardly see the day when such complex calculations as the fine-sheer of a garboard strake, from stem to stern-post, with eye-charming, audacious curvatures undreamed of elsewhere in any works of art, will be set down in copperplate with a pen and ink in a school exercise book, and put in order to last so beautifully for a hundred years and sometimes much longer. Tragically, except perhaps for some professional artists, we have mostly lost the habit of our grandfathers and grandmothers of intending things we are having made for us to last far beyond our own lifetimes. What of any charm or grace, are we, in the late 20th century, putting into the future, besides a few remnants of Victorian and other past ages?

A little further downstream on the River Thames, at Greenwich, lies, in a stone dry-dock, the famous tea-clipper *Cutty Sark*, built in Scotland. What modern sculptor can carve anything to match her intricate grace? What architect can hope to design any building to be as stirring, as impressive? What ancient Egyptian or Aztec pyramid can match her shape? What mighty Greek or Roman temple? What medieval cathedral? She, while beating them all in utter zest of form, also moved across the face of the waters for thousands of miles, sailing against the clock.

Westward, across the Atlantic Ocean, in the South Street Seaport, New York City, near the world's financial hub at Wall Street, rests *Wavertree*, the largest iron sailing ship in existence. She was built in 1885, in Southampton, England, for the jute trade between Britain and India, but later sailed on "tramp" (casual-trade) voyages world-wide. In 1910, *Wavertree* was dismasted in a terrific storm off Cape Horn, and condemned in the Falkland Islands, where she lay as a hulk until 1948, when she was towed to Buenos Aires and used as a sand barge. Then in 1968-70, she was towed to New York City and has been there on display ever since, under the shadow of the Wall Street skyscrapers. It is a fitting resting-place; many a current fortune was founded on ships like *Wavertree*.

Also in the South Street Seaport lies *Peking*. She was built in 1911 in Germany, to carry nitrate (guano) from Chile to Europe by way of Cape Horn. She was captured by the British from the Germans and used, in the '30s, as a school ship and has been in New York since 1965.

The United States has many more sailing ocean trade ships on display, including some recently-built craft in the old style: *Alexandria*, a Danish schooner built in 1928, now on display at Alexandria, Virginia; *American Eagle*, schooner, built 1930, now at Gloucester, Massachusetts; *Balclutha*, full-rigged ship, built 1886 in Scotland, and *C.A Thayer*, a three-masted schooner, built 1895 in California, both now in San Francisco; *Falls of Clyde*, four-masted, full-rigged ship, built 1878 in Scotland, now at Honolulu, Hawaii; *Moshulu*, four-masted barque, built 1904 in Scotland, now laid up in Camden, New Jersey; *Star of India*, built in the Isle of Man in 1863 for the New Zealand trade, a full-rigged ship, now at San Diego, California. There are many more sailing ships on display in the U.S., of course, but the ones I've mentioned are trading ships which were already famous in their own right in their day, long ago, in the ocean trade.

The further we pass in time from the age of working sail, the more wondrous all those long trading voyages, the vessels, and the men who sailed them appear to anyone who knows anything at all of the sea. It was and will be considered in future far more wonderful than the present air travel. Future generations will have to try to imagine a world when it was cheaper, quicker and more efficient, for example, to send ice blocks from Boston, Massachusetts 14,000 miles by sea all the way to Bombay, India, than it would have been to carve ice from the high mountains of the Himalayas and cart it by oxen only a few hundred miles overland. In 2194 AD, children will imagine a world where it was much more comfortable and convenient, in many instances quicker, and even comparatively safer, to travel in a ship by the trade winds' ways from London to Shanghai, China, by way of the Bay of Biscay, the South Atlantic Ocean, the Cape of Good Hope, the Indian Ocean and the East Indies, than it was, until the steam train came along, to travel overland or by river from say London to Kharkov. This, without these ships as witnesses, would be almost impossible for people in the future to appreciate. Considering the tremendous distances involved, and the almost complete lack of navigational aids apart from logs, a few—not always accurate—celestial tables and the brains and skills of good captains, mates, shipwrights, sailmakers and boatswains, practically every single one of those ocean trading voyages, through all the hazards and dangers of the seas, was a tremendous achievement. I like to think that in 2194 AD youngsters will try to imagine, for instance, the two tea clippers, *Ariel* and *Taiping*, leaving a Chinese port on the same tide, and arriving months later, after almost 20,000 miles ocean sailing, at the Thames estuary *within 20 minutes of each other* . . . having sighted each other, since they parted company off the coast of China, only once before reaching the English Channel.

When we now and in future think of how much more easily we travel, by air, land or sea, we should reflect on the courage, intelligence, and skills of our longshore and seafaring forebears, especially those in Victorian times. I suspect that a little of what I've mentioned must be, even vaguely, in the minds of many members of the public after a visit to a "museum sailing ship."

Sea-Change

By the early '60s, I'd been at sea pretty well since my 14th birthday, first before the war, as boy-deckie in a sailing-barge, then in the Royal Navy (lower deck) and from 1952 onwards, in what landspeople call "yachts," but what we always call "small craft." I was deck-hand, then mate, and then skipper. By 1959, I had my own craft, which I lived aboard and sailed in between yacht-delivery trips and any other work I might find. *Cresswell* was a converted wooden RNLI lifeboat, built in 1909; I'd bought her for £350.

Politically, like most British "matelots" of my generation on destroyers' messdecks, I'd picked up, by osmosis, *Labourite-Socialism*. In retrospect, what political ideas I had probably stemmed much more from 19th-century Working Men's Clubs than from Marx. After my medical discharge from the Service, I'd practically forgotten politics, because of the daily struggle to stay self-sufficient, free, and at sea.

Then, while in Sète, in southern France, through the sailing grapevine, I'd arranged by telegram a contract to deliver, starting three months later, a 40-foot ketch from Gibraltar to Brazil. My intention was to sail slowly down the Spanish coast, in order to find a berth in Gibraltar for my boat while I was away from her. Berths in Gib were charged for, unlike in Spanish harbors.

I'd started to cast off the lines from Sète jetty when the young Englishman appeared. It was towards dusk (always minions of the moon, we sailors) and I was anxious to get well clear of the French coast before dark. I was alone and it was before the time of automatic steering gears. The weather signs were good, but the prospect of being at the helm for hours was gloomy. I'd worked hard all day re-rigging the mast. I would sail out clear until the small hours, then when dawn broke I'd snatch a few hours of sleep with my boat drifting.

"Where are you sailing?"

I hadn't heard my own language for weeks. I looked up. He was English—no doubt about that. One of the bulldog breed, I knew as soon as I saw his face. He wore a large khaki traveling coat and had a small rucksack slung over his shoulder. Around his neck hung two camera cases.

"Spain . . . Barcelona . . ."

Departure time is not for idle chatter.

"Can I come along?"

He was in his early twenties, short, stubby, and looked clean and healthy enough. It was before the spread of illegal drugs made such "pier-head" enlistments inadvisable. It would be much better to sail *Cresswell* direct to Barcelona without stopping and drifting for sleep. It was autumn; there was always the threat of a sudden mistral wind blowing up.

"Ever sailed?" I asked.

"In a dinghy once or twice."

I'd heard that one at least a hundred times from would-be crew.

"Cook?"

"Well . . . yep."

"Okay, chuck your bag aboard. You can share the helm after I show you the ropes."

The young man introduced himself as John. He was not talkative, and I liked that. By dusk, John was showing himself to be a handy fast-learner. By midnight, he was on the helm with orders to stay on compass course and to wake me should anything at all turn up; if the wind should increase, or if he saw any light.

An hour before dawn, after John woke me with a cooked breakfast, we were well on the way to becoming, not friends, but something even better in a small craft at sea: *used to avoiding one another*.

Despite lack of any real wind, we managed to potter into Barcelona the following evening. Then there were no yacht marinas; we berthed wherever there was a convenient space. I chose to go alongside the city jetty close by the model of Columbus' *Santa Maria* near to the harbor-end of the Ramblas de Las Flores. Under the docklamps' glare, we were inspected by two Guardia Civiles, in grey uniforms and shiny black leather hats, rifles slung over their shoulders. Both looked uninterested enough.

I'd asked John for his passport, and with both his and mine in hand addressed the policemen. My Spanish by then was quite good.

"Buenas noches, Señores. Quieremos entrar en España y iremos al restaurante." ("Good evening, we wish to enter Spain and go to a restaurant.").

The elder of the two Guardia Civiles shook his head.

"Es muy tarde" ("It's very late . . .")

I switched on my lean look.

"Tenemos hambre, Señores!" ("We're hungry.")

The senior Guardia Civil wafted his free hand in the direction of the dock-gate.

"Muchas gracias, Señores!"

As I landed on the jetty, I handed John back his passport, and to the Guardia Civil's polite "Muy buenos apetitos," we headed for the gate.

The first thing John did when we came to the wide Ramblas de Las Flores was search among the news vendors' stalls for a London "Times" newspaper. It took quite a while, but he finally sighted one and bought it. It was a week old, but he only wanted the crossword puzzle, he said. I was accustomed to oddballs among sailing crews, so did not object to our delay.

The little café we finally entered was dirty but cheap, not far from the dock-gates. It seemed to be full of poorly-dressed deaf mutes sitting and gazing blankly. We were the only diners. The only expressions to be seen were of plain old suffering, except for the fat café-owner. His look somehow managed to combine both suffering and avarice. As we ate, one lottery vendor, one beggar after another, approached our table, the old, the young, the lame, the blind. They were all shushed away by the café-owner. When we had eaten and as we finished our wine, John laid his "Times" out on the table and set to work on the crossword.

While he was thus occupied, I stared into my tobacco-smoke. The café-owner was absent. A young woman, clean, but dressed in black rags, approached, a baby held close to her. I'd been around the ports of the world, and I'd learned to ignore the more egregious frauds who chose to beg. But this gaunt woman had that look in her eyes that comes only from real starvation. She could have been twenty or thirty, or even forty: there comes a time of such worn despair that age means nothing. As she held her palm out over our table, John, who was bent frowning over his puzzle, gestured her away with one hand. At the same time, I delved in my pocket and dragged out a tattered note—it could not have been more than ten pesetas, and offered it the young woman, who dropped to her knees and kissed my hand.

Although I'm from Wales, I've never liked public displays of emotion. I beckoned the young mother to stand. She did so, and, murmuring "Dios te bendito, Señor!" she turned to leave the café.

My companion did not look up from his crossword puzzle; his voice was low and cold and flat.

"You know that kind of thing will block the revolution."

I thought he was joking. It didn't strike home then, but I must have replied: "Well . . . a kid to feed . . ."

And that was the end of that, and as we walked back to the boat to the night calls of the *serenos* (night-watchmen), it didn't mean much, nor did it for quite a long time.

One of a yacht-captain's jobs is to see that all customs' routines are carried out properly. In these days, this is made easier by computers; in the old days it was a pain in the neck, usually a traipse from one office to another with bundles of forms, and with no English speaker within miles.

I awoke early next day to find my crewman missing. I dashed ashore and searched around the empty docks for a while; there was no sign of John. I dared not report that to the gate-office; I would probably be arrested for aiding an illegal entrant. I didn't know if the Guardia Civiles of the previous night had reported *Cresswell*'s arrival or not. If they had, I'd be arrested because my crew was missing; if they had not, and John was apprehended ashore, and told the police he'd arrived in *Cresswell*, I'd be arrested. Whichever way, I'd wind up in a cell.

There's an old sailors' saw, *"When in danger or in doubt, hoist the sail and head off out."* I quietly slipped my docklines and, by daylight, was a mile down the sea-channel out of Barcelona, headed for Majorca. There were no computers, and it would take ages for an alarm to reach Majorca, if one was raised by the Spanish dock police.

As I headed for the offing, as one tends to, I thought of the recent events, and remembered that when my crew had handed me his passport the evening before, I'd caught a peep of his name. It didn't mean much to me then, but I never forget a name. His was *Philby*.

It took me another two years to discover that John Philby had been a working cameraman on Fleet Street. I still don't know if he showed his passport formally to enter Spain, nor if the Guardia Civil found his name of interest. I wonder if in fact I smuggled Kim Philby's son (I saw a picture of the temporary crewman later: there's no doubt that's who he was) into Franco's Spain.

Whether I did or not, that one remark in that dirty café had swung my compass needle right around. From the moment John Philby spoke then, I've never believed in pie-in-the-sky.

Previously published in The Salisbury Review (1993)

Splendid Remembrances

It's said that when you drown all your life passes before you. I don't know, although I've been very close to drowning often in years of sail voyaging in small craft. What I do know now though, as in my fading my life passes before me in slower motion than perhaps at a drowning, is that the three most splendid things I ever did were not done under sail at all—not even done at sea.

The first splendid thing was to pierce the Iron Curtain on *May 1*, 1985, in my ocean-trimaran *Outward Leg* on the river Danube. I'd spent the previous winter in thick ice on the river Main, fighting German bureaucracy, which in the end side-tracked me to Ingoldstadt; then I'd wended downstream on the Upper Danube to Vienna and waited there for three weeks. The waiting was no pain. I couldn't afford the Opera but I had invitations to dinners, while being entranced (courtesy of the Oberbürgermeister) at Vienna Boys Choir concerts: it was like hearing the salute of angels.

On the river Danube itself, apart from two patrol-boats manned by rather handsome but perplexed-looking, Kalashnikov-waving, youths in green sailor's hats and collars, there was little sign of the Iron Curtain. Ashore were watchtowers, of course, and barbed wire fading away over distant hills.

Inside Czechoslovakia, the first sign of May Day was the loom beyond a distant bend, through misty rain, of a huge

Ferris wheel. As we neared I saw that it was moving slowly and had a big red star at its axle, slowly revolving.

I'd acquired *Outward Leg* in San Diego, California, where she was registered, so astern she wore, of course, her U.S. ensign. Amidships, over my head, she wore my British Red Duster. Both ensigns were about as big as king-size bedsheets. She wore also a big Red Dragon flag of Wales and a small pennant of Bavaria, for my German crew Thomas Ettenhuber (may he rest in peace!). There's sound reason in this (to nonriver folk) poncy-seeming flag-flaunting: on heavily trafficked rivers, crews in other vessels notice you quicker. Underway on bendy rivers I played over a tape loudspeaker, as loud as possible, airs on Scottish bagpipes. Again with good reason; anyone in a rowing boat will hear and, if they've any sense, get out of the way. In any case, I like bagpipes; I wouldn't sail with a crew who don't, so on the ocean they bother no one else. All in all, with her mast down on deck, her ensigns bristling, her bagpipes blasting, *Outward Leg* with her three low hulls must have looked like some praying mantis strayed from a jubilee party.

Through drizzle, we rounded a wide bend of the Danube. Over the far, shallow riverbank, hovered ancient, elegant houses and palaces, ugly factories and workers' tower-flats all jumbled together. On our side, where the deep channel was, only inches away from my boat as she passed at about five knots, spread a big city park. Its funfair was crowded, mostly by uniformed soldiers. There were thousands of them. Soviets were by far in the majority.

Even as we passed under the main Bratislava city road bridge, I saw that the shadows beneath the bridge were crowded with senior officers sheltering from the rain. There were a good hundred of them, mostly Soviet; majors, colonels, generals, you name it. On the narrow pavement above the riverbank, in dank gloom they were lined up, grimly, as if on a podium for a Red Square review. *Outward Leg* passed them by—an egregious symbol of individual freedom—and she left each one of them, one by one, astern; their shoes polished, pants baggy, epaulettes exhausted, medals adroop, jaws agape, eyes apop; astounded was hardly the word for it.

Astonishment had struck the air like a whiplash. I'd looked right into eyes as we passed and sensed: *one lone leaf was drifting along a gutter—a hundred-thousand leaves would break it.* Imagine: it had been as if an albatross had glided very low over Wormwood Scrubs.

When we merged from under that bridge the Ferris wheel was still, its red star faded in the rain.

The KGB were never slow. Next day's events indicate that they probably tried, through the river police, to arrange the sinking of *Outward Leg*—but that's another story.

My second splendid thing happened a few days later, on May 8, 1985. It was VE Day and my birthday. Hungarian police had chased me up and down the Danube for four days. Worn out, they finally allowed *Outward Leg*, to the waves and blown kisses of thousands ashore, to moor right alongside the Ministry of the Interior (read, then, "secret police") on Roosevelt Square hard by the beautiful (but copied) English Adam Clarke chain-bridge.

I stayed there, all flags flying, for three weeks. In those twenty-one days, if one person made the "V" sign to me, a hundred thousand did. In Budapest I played the bagpipes low, for myself and maybe for what was bound to happen.

In Budapest, on May 10, 1985, I reported the arrival of *Outward Leg* to the U.S. Consulate. I was almost thrown out in the staff's haste to avoid "awkward incidents."

My third splendid remembrance is of the end of my Danube voyage, in the Romanian Black Sea port of Constanta. I'd seen at very close quarters, right through Ceausescu's domain, everything that the West now knows about—and a lot more besides. I'd seen enough aged folk forced to fish for hours in rain on soggy riverbanks and turn in a catch before they might eat; enough half-starved, barefoot kids stealing scraps of awful grub in filthy "Workers' Restaurants;" enough forced labor on the Black Sea Canal; enough sacrifice to build a useless shipping port on sand.

On July 6, 1985, at the Terazza Cafe, in Port Tomis, then a haunt of Constanta Communist Party officials, I stood and, in my very best French so they would understand, told 300 of them that Nicolai Ceausescu—and they—were bloody-handed oligarchs, and that they would not prevail.

I was thrown out of Romania, of course. But in 1990 I was invited back—as Commodore of a projected Constanta yacht marina. It didn't take long for me to realize that the old gang, with all its corruption, was still in charge. So I left Romania again, but this time of my own volition.

My book *The Improbable Voyage* came out in 1987. My ten previous voyaging books must have been (although unconsciously) "politically correct," especially after my run-ins with Boer bullies in the '70s. But for *The Improbable Voyage*, there were hardly any notices in the U.K. press. A couple of critics snarled that I had been "looking for trouble so I could write about it." Later, Rod Heikell, a "yacht-guide" hack, wo'd wafted down the Danube in Soviet ferries in '85, and who obviously doesn't know Marx from Donald Duck, wrote that I had exaggerated the obstacles on my Danube voyage and that I had been provocative, by for instance wearing my boat's national ensign and my own flag through five communist countries—on an international waterway. I wonder: did these poor wretches never know the joy of cocking a snook at bullies from the safety of their father's shadow? Of course I provoked bullies. Of course I cocked a snook at them. But, to paraphrase Winston Churchill—and surely no exaggeration: *Some bullies—some cock—some snook!*

Previously published in The Salisbury Review (1992)

Resting

I wrote this short, previously unpublished piece immediately upon the arrival of *Outward Leg* in Thailand in June 1986. Two months later, after finishing my book *Somewheres East of Suez*, I was at work training disabled young Thais to be achievers. Thank God again and again I have succeeded with each one I have taken aboard. In each instance, it was a greater thing than any ocean crossing I ever made.

I showed this piece to several friends at the time. After the political events of 1989-91 in Eastern Europe, they all asked me how it was that I had been so sure in 1986 that the Communist Empire was rotting, and about to fall. I told them in the same way that I know when the tide is going out.

I've always said that anyone who does not feel capable, physically, mentally, or for any other reason, of continuing a voyage without the risk of becoming a burden to others, should stop and rest, at least until he or she does feel absolutely confident about pressing on. I've never had any doubts about this; in my mind it is one of the irrefutable laws of the sea. One of the things I learned long ago is that it takes courage to be a seeming coward; but in the matter of long-distance voyage making, we can—indeed we should—discount any of the landsmen's conceptions about the abstract notion of "heroism." There's no such thing as a hero at sea; there are only the wise, fools, and irresponsible "romantics," many of whom end up putting other good people's lives at risk.

Exhaustion, physical or psychological, among small craft sailors on long voyages is, it seems, a subject hardly yet researched by anyone in a scientific manner. That it does occur, and more frequently than we like to admit, is a fact of life. Another fact is that its recognition is a great cure for any incipient "machismo" or "elitism."

Enough of giving you a prod towards an avenue of deep thought; I'll get to the nub of the matter and tell you that by the time I reached Thailand I was exhausted.

It's no sin to feel very tired at age 62 and on one leg. If it were, I would probably try to excuse myself, but excuses never got anyone off a lee shore, so I may as well just state baldly: by the time *Outward Leg* reached Thailand, I was, as the old saying goes, "ragged, bagged, and shagged." Reasons are—well, more reasonable—than excuses, and there were good reasons for my feeling knackered. For a start, I'd navigated almost 25,000 miles since leaving San Diego in late '83, visited 28 different countries, written two books, been fobbed of again by the British establishment (working-class upstart—and Welsh, too!), made the first-ever crossing of Europe by the Rhine-Danube route in an ocean multihull (simultaneously cocking an ocean-snook at the Red Army in their rusting, tottering southeastern European Empire), and refitted the damage caused by KGB nefarious intent; and all on a shoestring; and one shoestring, not two.

"Enough's enough—for the time being," I thought, when we arrived in Thailand. "Time for a rest." Anyone who cannot recognize their own signs of exhaustion is heading for a fall (Soviets included). I've seen it happen time and time again, to other people, in my wanderings over the years.

But there was something else bugging me besides exhaustion when we arrived in Phuket. Ever since I'd hauled out of San Diego almost three years before, I'd been questioning my line of intent, and my course was throughout gradually changing. Solo voyages, extended, are a bore in the long run, not only for the persons who make them, but also for

everyone else, eventually. The same goes for setting solo ex-
amples, and I know what I'm saying; I've done them both
aplenty. It has to do with the only thing that's worthwhile
about being alone . . . and that's being, at the same time, *creative*. Being alone without being creative is merely an ordeal.
I've never enjoyed it; it's always been forced upon me by circumstances.

I'd left California to sail east around the world north of
the Equator—by far, I am still convinced, the most arduous
sailing circumnavigational route in every way—to give an example to other amputees as to what they might do given the
means. It was all baloney, of course. It's better to personally
help one cripple to launch a dinghy, than to hammer oceans
alone or even with a few others.

Better to give one limbless kid ten minutes of our time
than conquer alone all the world's oceans. Through that one
limping kid, maybe not directly, but by God's own paths and
even through eons of time, we might *conquer the stars.*

PART

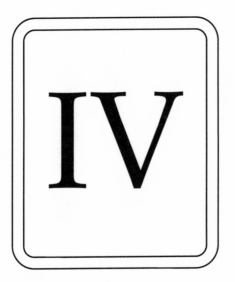

IV

Back to the Sea

One of the special things about sailing in small craft is that when you're in trouble, are perhaps injured, and suppose you ought to be feeling sorry for yourself, you discover that you aren't. I have always known this, but it came back to me very forcefully this past year. Instead of going on my arranged delivery of a Freedom 40 from Florida to California, my first major ocean passage in a number of years and a calculated "return to the sea" after being a landbound writer, I found myself in a New York City hospital with my left leg amputated just below the thigh. There's no need to go into reasons here. Solutions are always more interesting to a sailor than problems.

But once out, I was astonished to discover, when SAIL published a small piece on my "misfortune," how many sailors there were in the New York area. Although I've lived in New York on and off for the past six years, I have never consciously sought out the locals. But here they were, telephoning and writing to wish me a swift recovery and offering to take me sailing when I was well enough. I wanted to go very much, but there were things that needed attending to—mainly dealing with both an artificial limb and my feelings about what had happened to me, as well as trying to come to terms with the physical pain.

By the end of April, I finally collected my modern miracle leg. It was a beauty, smooth as a midshipman's cheeks and ten times more shapely than its mate. It also bent at the knee by means of a stainless steel spring cleverly hidden inside the lower leg. "What a great idea," I thought, "if we could build masts like that: fold the top half down at the spreaders and get rid of all that tophamper in a bad blow." (I've said it before, and I'll keep saying it: the next really major improvement in safety at sea in small craft will be reducing tophamper conveniently when hove-to in bad weather.)

Shortly after I'd become accustomed to walking around on the plastic-steel wonder, Peggy arrived. She stole my heart away just as swiftly as my old boat *Sea Dart* had done on the first day I clapped eyes on her in Bequia nine years ago. Lin and Larry Pardey had asked me for my measurements so they could make a leg for me from the balk of timber from which the stem of their new boat was being fashioned. I must confess I imagined something a bit crude, as in the pictures we have seen of old-time sailormen. I should have known better. A bit crude? From California?

When I first saw Peggy, she was superb—about twenty-seven inches high with a freeboard flattened on four sides. From there on down, the leg is absolutely round and all hollow. Oh, the craftiness of those wooden boatbuilders. Peggy is 3½ pounds lighter than the plastic and steel counterpart.

Into the leg's socket I fitted a plaster mold made in St. Vincent's Hospital. This I secured with through bolts, the heads of which are concealed under inlaid silver coins of Britain and Holland, while just above the leg my pants are held in place by a leather strap decorated with silver coins of Canada and the United States (and a French one for my friend, Bernard Moitessier). On the front socket "flat" part just below the "knee," I have fitted a fish carved out of whalebone in the 1850s by the Nantucket great-grandfather of a lady friend. Around part of the outside of the socket, there will be fitted a four-inch brass plate giving the history of this marvelous timber—a true throwback to the sailing days of yore.

Meanwhile, my good friend Dean Cycon, a New York attorney, called on me. I was busy with the draft of a very long new book. A first draft is a sacrosanct beast. It owns my whole soul. So, absentmindedly I stared at Dean as he asked me if I wanted to go sailing.

I ought to explain here that amputees, especially those who have had much pain before their operation, often suffer from a strange phenomenon, about which the medical profession knows very little. It's called "phantom-limb pain," and for the first few months after the operation, at least, it can be excruciating. I had decided that I would just have to accept the pain and learn to live with it. It hadn't been easy, but after a while I began feeling when the pain was not there that I missed it. When that happened, it helped me remember that no storm lasts forever.

I stared at Dean in silence while hot electric pains tore through calf muscles that were no longer there. He repeated, "Do you want to go sailing, Tris? I've got a boat lined up for you whenever you want to go. A nice 64-footer, *Ventura*."

I can't say truthfully that the pain disappeared right away. All I know is that my heart leaped, and I had to make an effort to sound casual when I replied, "When?"

"Tomorrow from Pier 11."

"Right, Dean. You're on."

A lot of people write to me and tell me that they have been sailing lately. It usually goes something like this: "It was only two weeks, nothing like the voyages you have made, of course. I expect it sounds trite and boring to you . . ." How wrong they are!

Every time someone sets off under sail, no matter the distance, he or she is making an endeavor to reach for the infinite.

Ventura was working as a day-charter boat, although this winter she'll be heading down to the Virgins for the charter season there. The sail I was to have in her, ten weeks and a day after I left the operating table, was only around New York Harbor—to the south of the Battery, out to Ellis and Liberty islands, and back around Governors Island. It was only to be "a trip around the lighthouse," as the ocean sailors, the deep-water lads and lassies, would put it.

But to me, the moment I hobbled down to the floating dock and somehow clambered onto *Ventura* as she plunged and rose in the wake of passing tugs and barges, it was an odyssey. I never had a more personally hazardous, and certainly never a sweeter, voyage, even though the wind never raised itself above 18 knots or so. Its direction was steady as that of a dockside wall, east-southeast by south.

After a half hour, Peggy settled down enough for me to wander forward and aft. For a half hour, I even took the wheel, and there was no finer way to test my new sea leg than bearing off the wind, shoving a stiff wheel as it steered the 50-odd (waterline) feet of hull under me.

Ventura had a mixed crew of lawyers, dentists, office workers, and students on board for two hours. But as we shoved off and the sails were hoisted, I felt I had earned the right to let my imagination go. To me, as she sailed into the harbor, she was a carrack of gold bearing jeweled gifts of homage to the gods of the sea. The mists around the lofty towers of the World Trade Center were the lambswool trade-wind clouds around the high peak of Tenerife.

It's going to be a long job to become as agile on board as I once was, but as we get older we may all say that. I mustn't allow myself, I decided, to believe that I'm at all special or different. It's what's left that matters, and that's what I discovered on my sail "around the lighthouse."

I got so caught up in the sailing that I did something in *Ventura* that I don't think I've ever done before, at least not that I can remember. We were running free, wind and wing behind Governors Island, in a pretty narrow channel. The main gybed. The mainsheet caught itself up in a "soldier's knot" around its own winch.

I had been standing, as best I could, abaft the helmsman.

Without thinking twice, if at all, I made a sudden dash for the sheet to free it. Of course, I went over—bows first. I managed to break my fall on the after coachroof, just abaft the main-sheet winch. That was when the mainsheet thwacked me right on my spine and knocked me flying.

Fortunately, I landed on my good leg and so prevented any harm to Peggy. It took me a few seconds to gather myself together; my back stung and I was cursing like a drayman, but I was secretly pleased.

To have done what I did so unawares, to dash forward and make a grab for the mainsheet to free it, meant only one thing, and for me it was the best thing in the world. It meant that I had, for a few blessed moments, completely forgotten my pain and reacted instinctively to the problem as a true sailor should.

And as for self-pity, it never helped anyone beat off a lee shore, did it?

Previously published in SAIL (1982)

Across the Kra

In October 1983, I sailed in my 40-foot trimaran *Outward Leg* from San Diego, on a "very long voyage." It was 18 months after my left leg had been amputated above the knee. My intention was to show to other amputees, and especially youngsters, by my own example, what they were capable of, given the proper motivation. I headed south to the Pacific Ocean, east through the Panama Canal, then to Colombia and Venezuela. From there, I headed north to New York, and so across the Atlantic Ocean to Britain.

By October 1984, when I reached London and set off to cross Europe by the Rhine-Danube route (and incidentally to take the first private yacht behind the Iron Curtain), I had realized that my original intent was futile. To put it simply, the vast majority of disabled people, young or old, in this world will never even get within hailing distance of a modern, state-of-the-art ocean sailing craft, multihulled or not, leave alone sail in one. I concluded that I must go among them, in their own environment, and, using the resources that were more easily available to them, teach them to overcome and achieve.

We needed a challenge, preferably boating, which had never before been successfully beaten by anyone else, which would be just—and only just—within the physical capabilities of crippled youngsters, and yet would not take them more than twenty-four hours away from medical assistance should it be needed. It would have to be something that could be done cheaply; we were not sponsored; we had to do it all on

our own. The last proviso was that the successful feat, whatever it would be, must be of some use to others, disabled or
not.

In the New York Public Library I searched . . .

By the time *Outward Leg* left Istanbul, I had reckoned
where and what the challenge was: to cross by boat for the
first time in recorded history, the Isthmus of Kra, in Thailand.

In July 1986, *Outward Leg* fetched west Thailand . . .

The first question was, of course, could there be a river
passage across the Kra? According to the world's foremost ge-
ographical authorities—no. Maps and charts of the area were
very inaccurate or non-existent. Satellite photographs showed
only cloud formations of the vapor risen from thick jungle.
Most Thais ridiculed the idea—even though a waterway
across the Isthmus has been a national dream for centuries.
Some Thais held that ancient legends said that Chinese boats,
eons ago, passed over the Isthmus.

I was accompanied by Thomas Ettenhuber, a young German who had joined *Outward Leg* in Nuremberg in December
1985. The first thing was for Thomas and for me, as far as possible on one leg, to explore the Isthmus by land. This meant
adapting a motorcycle and me learning to drive it on rough
tracks. This we did in spasms of frantic—and for me painful—
activity during the dry season, October-March 1986-87.

As I had suspected, and as in the Panama Isthmus, there
is a valley across the Isthmus of Kra running north and south,
and in that valley are two rivers, one, the Mae Nam Trang,
running south into the Andaman Sea; the other, the Mae Nam
Ta Pi, north into the Gulf of Thailand. These, in the southwest
monsoon rainy season, join over the watershed. If we could
get to the headwaters of the south-running river, the Trang, by
the start of the monsoon rains, before the channel over the
watershed became a raging torrent, we would stand a chance
of navigating the whole way across the Kra.

In our "spare time"—do sailors ever have any?—between

bouts of exploring the Isthmus, we found a suitable boat and trained our crew of young Thais: Som, nineteen, one arm; Anant, fourteen, one leg; and Nok, fourteen, cleft palate/mastoid. We taught them basic English, hull and engine maintenance, and persistence. Stoicism and a wonderful sense of humor were theirs already.

Our boat was a twenty-year-old Similan Island open longtail fishing boat, 40 feet LOA, seven-foot beam, and one-foot-three-inches draft, built solidly of an iroko-like wood. Buying her bare hull set our Atlantis Society back £300. Refurbishing the hull and fitting monsoon-rain shelters cost another 50 quid or so. An eleven-horsepower longtail diesel engine was generously provided free by the Yanmar Company of Japan, who also supplied a spare seven-horsepower diesel engine as an emergency standby. By late May of 1987, all was ready. The monsoon rains were due to start about mid-June. Our D-Day was, fittingly, June 6th.

We headed out to cross 100 miles of shallow, rough Andaman Sea on a dead lee shore. With our Yanmar eleven-horsepower longtail engine, *Henry Wagner*, at 85 percent full speed, could make ten knots. But rough seas, of course, slowed us down. Even so, we pounded so much that we lost our eight-horsepower dinghy-outboard and a small anchor over the side. It was a wonder to see how one-armed Som, and one-legged Anant managed to balance themselves in that rough sea. Our first call was at the islet of Ko Mai Thon—little more than a bare rock with a few palm trees, with a poor anchorage. Then to the (then still-unspoiled) beautiful island of Ko Phi Phi. One night anchored there, and then we were right off the beaten tourist tracks of South Thailand.

The charts were old and almost laughably inaccurate. They had islands where there were none, and no islands where there might be a dozen or so . . . We eyeballed our way in heavy rain into the lee of Ko Lanta Yai, surely, when the rain cleared, one of the most beautiful vistas on Earth, where we were told that we were the first foreigners to visit there in our

own craft since the Imperial Japanese Army departed after
World War II . . .

It took us three days to reach Kantang, on the mouth of
the River Trang, from Phuket. Three days of very heavy steering. Remember that with a longtail we were not merely
swinging a tiller, but the whole engine.

Every night, in those remote anchorages, we kept a look-
out for other craft anchored near us. If one came we would
shift to another anchorage, well clear. On the whole, the Thai
fishermen were friendly. We still kept our distance. Smugglers
were much in evidence, with longtail craft of up to 60 feet
LOA, fitted with powerful truck-engines, capable of making
over thirty knots.

One more night at anchor in breezeless, humid, Kantang,
plagued by mosquitoes, despite our nets, and by the continual
noise of fishing craft coming and going. Early the next day, almost light-heartedly, we set off up the River Trang, only
guessing a mite of what lay before us; thirty days of obdurate
obstacles, immense effort, awful heat and always high humidity. We kept careful records on our portable computer.

The River Trang itself, as well as its banks, was snake-
infested. Many of these were poisonous. We had to be awake
to this danger all the time. Fortunately, no one was bitten. At
Trang, about twenty miles inland, we moored off a monastery,
to be told we were the first foreigners ever seen there. Apprentice monks, boys from six to sixteen, crowded round us,
silently curious.

A mile or so above Trang, the river narrowed and became
shallower. There a huge tree was fallen right across the river,
blocking our way forward. The girth of the trunk was about
fifteen feet. We set to and sawed the trunk through twice by
hand, and rolled the cut section out of the way using tackles.
It took half a day to clear that tree. Then we rounded the next
bend upstream and found another fallen tree . . . We didn't
know then, of course, that by the time we finally reached the
Gulf of Thailand we would have cut and shifted, all by hand,

38 full-size fallen trees, innumerable smaller ones, about 160 tons of rock from the rapids and we would have lifted our 1.2-ton boat manually over 120 times.

The distance across the Kra Isthmus, north to south, is about 120 kilometers. The rivers twisted and turned so much, every which way, that the total distance covered by *Henry Wagner* was about 480 kilometers. By mid-June, we were halfway to the headwaters of the River Trang, and making about twenty kilometers a day; but the water was shallowing hourly; still there was no sign of the monsoon rains. This was worrying; here was a trap. If the monsoon did break heavily, with our boat between the high banks of the Trang, the river would swiftly become a raging storm drain, and *Henry Wagner*, most probably with us in her, would surely be swept to destruction. We simply had to keep moving forward, to reach a place where we might, if the rains broke suddenly and fiercely, haul the boat safely out of the river.

By late June, we were almost at the watershed, at our highest altitude, on this crossing, of thirty meters above sea level, near the provincial capital of Thung Song. Now we had run out of river water almost completely; we had been reduced to painfully dragging the boat along the river-bed by hand or with blocks and tackles from tree to tree. There was yet another sixteen kilometers to go over a rocky, almost wholly obstacle-littered river-bed before we could reach a riverbank gradient that was not too steep to haul up the boat to comparative safety.

Both Thomas and I were by this time covered with festering sores from scratches caused by thorns. They simply would not heal, and caused us much sleeplessness at night.

By this time, we were felling trees downstream of us to block what trickle of water there was, to raise the level around the boat—in effect building a canal as we progressed painfully and slowly. We felled a total of fourteen trees in this way. We encountered 122 fish traps, which we dismantled before we passed through them, and rebuilt when we had done. We also dismantled 148 low foot-bridges and rebuilt them after our passing.

No tractor, no truck, no crane, could possibly reach us. I even considered lifting the boat out of the river-bed by helicopter; but even if there had been one available, there was no chance of doing this safely because of densely overhanging trees. There was only one solution, and I knew that it existed, because in my motorbike rambles I had spied him . . . the only working elephant in south Thailand. There was no intention to hold a circus, no rodomontade about our solution; the plain fact was that the only way we could save the boat from the risk of being swept away by a sudden flash flood was with an elephant.

The elephant was intelligent. If he came to an outcrop of rock or a fallen tree, he would either kick it aside or dredge it out of the way with his immense head. Our elephant—his name was Tong Chai (Fluttering Banner)—was forty years old. His mahout had obtained him cheaply, he said, because Tong Chai had killed two men the month before on a rubber plantation. But he told me this after I'd made pals with Tong Chai, and fed him half a pound of sugar . . .

Tong Chai, once he was sure that the boat was not some kind of threat to him, hauled *Henry Wagner* steadily and sedately for sixteen kilometers in three days. Like any good trade unionist, he did not strain himself more than necessary and would take his time to think his way around a fallen tree or an outcrop of boulders.

When we finally reached the main road to Thung Song, Thomas and I left *Henry Wagner*. Taking our rubber dinghy with us and three days' supplies, we set off to follow the course of the river-bed. Most of the way, there were a few inches of water, but very often we had to drag the dinghy, until we finally reached the headwaters of the River Mae Nam Ta Pi, which runs north to the Gulf of Thailand. Then we strapped the dinghy on top of a local bus and headed back for *Henry Wagner*.

The Thai Fourth Army was generous; it provided a crane and a truck, and hauled our boat twenty kilometers over the watershed, so that we could launch her into the Mae Nam Ta Pi.

From where we joined the Ta Pi, as the crow flies, it was about fifty kilometers to the Gulf of Thailand at Surat Thani. But on the twisting river, still cluttered with fallen trees and gravel banks, we covered 180 kilometers . . . in four days. The current was strong; about five knots, and the way we tackled the gravel banks, with no more than a couple of inches of water over them, was to rush at them full pelt, so raising a big wake-wave astern of us, and then, as we came to the bank, slow the engine right down, so that the wake-wave overtook the boat and lifted her, sometime for a quarter of a mile, hopefully right over the bank into the deeper water beyond.

The River Ta Pi was much wider than the River Trang. It was one of the most beautiful rivers I have ever seen, but even more beautiful was the first sight of the sea at the end of our thirty-day haul across the Kra Isthmus.

We in *Henry Wagner* did this Kra crossing to inspire our fellow-disabled. If you know someone who is disabled, and they don't know of what we did, will you please tell them?

On Dogs and Compassion

Jambo, my dog, is two and a half years old. He's from a Rawai litter whose father is about the laziest, fattest, ugliest, most disdainful, sneering old street-dog in Thailand—and that's saying something. Jambo has one beautiful sister and four neurotic-looking brothers who hang about casting lost, mournful looks at passing *farangs*. Maybe they know something I don't. I don't know Jambo's mother but she must be pretty; he himself is handsome indeed. He's a marvelous runner (up to forty kilometers per hour for short bursts). He's clever, can understand about ten orders in both Thai and English, ruinously charming, exceedingly artful, shockingly cunning, disgustingly gluttonous, and a reluctant swimmer.

Jambo shares with me an affection for children, he is good company, and he likes to be taught proper manners. His company is the best occasional therapy for a mind under stress. Jambo probably cannot understand my words as words, but he understands, I'm sure, my emotion as I speak them.

The other day I was driving along behind Wat Rawai, returning from Jambo's daily run—I won't say where or it might get crowded with dog runners. Ahead of us, where the paved road turns into a dirt-track, three dogs were, as usual at that spot, lying in ambush for us to pass so they could—naturally—chase us, barking. I was instructing Jambo on the proper response of a British sailor's dog—to ignore them.

"Keep your eyes on the f . . . road!" I told him in time-honored sailor's vernacular.

As I did so, we passed an hitherto anonymous, but with hindsight insipid-looking, *farang* riding a motorbike. He must have thought I had been addressing him. "F . . . off!" He bawled. So I did, fast. With both legs off above the knees, physical vulnerability is not the word for it.

Later the (evidently same) *farang* sent me a garbled message seeming to accuse me of all sorts of things, including hypocrisy—I'd recently criticized fast drivers over dirt-roads near houses. He also wrote that I am "pitiful" and must be "very lonely."

Those words, addressed to a man of 70 recovering from three severe operations might have hurt some. Not me. To me they're utterly stupid. My response to them has been learned the hard way. I had my first inklings of it over thirty years ago when I was beset in the Arctic ice cap—alone with a dog—for eighteen months.

Pity is a selfish exercise. It is felt or bestowed by those who are afraid of what may be in store for themselves. *Loneliness* is not a natural feeling. It is taught, mostly by those wishing to gain, usually either power or money, by preaching or selling something that will "cure our loneliness."

Compassion is a facet of love—it is felt by both the bestower and the recipient. It also comes with company.

Oh, surrounded as I am, even by good people—for a whole day of precious solitude!

Under Sail Again

In late 1992, in Phuket, besides speeding around ashore on my self-adapted motorcycle-wheelchair and at sea in *Little Legend*, I got hold of a full-size yacht, a Gougeon Brothers-designed, 42-foot, sloop-rigged catamaran, to be exact. How I got her is too complex and incredible (even eerie) for the average shore-side reader, and as I don't want to be accused of "stretching the truth," I'll settle here for a standing fact: in the fall of 1992, with the help of God, *I got our yacht.*

My diet is based on potatoes and oats, both of which are available locally, as well as wheat bread. The potatoes are grown in the north of Thailand where it's cooler. Boiled potatoes or chips with fish, chicken or prawns, fried, boiled or roasted. My main minder, Prasert, sometimes mixes for me raw oats with yogurt and fruit in season, for a kind of muesli. I take one aspirin a day on doctor's orders to "keep my veins clear." Other than that my only medicine is a sleeping pill, which I miss sometimes. I drink tea copiously, with milk and sugar. At evening, I drink Ovaltine. I often drink orange juice with my supper.

As I did today, I rise at dawn each morning. My main exercise each day is swinging myself off and onto my bed, and every morning and afternoon in the dry season, onto my *samlor* (motorcycle-sidecar combination), together with any pulling myself on and off and around boats. My bike rides and boat work jiggle my body, which I hope will keep my

169

liver well and my stomach muscles moving. Other than that, I normally go to bed with the sun, and then I turn myself from side to side about every five minutes for five hours until I fall asleep about eleven o'clock. I can't sit up to watch TV as I get "bottle" (a tiresome pain caused by weak stomach muscles). I read much, but less than I did, as I must save my eyes to write.

My physical therapy I've found out for myself, mainly by trial and error. My own fault: I'm scared that a doctor might try to slow me down, especially afloat, and so stop me from shoving, pushing and hauling to my limits. In any case, "If it ain't broke, don't fix it."

On December 16th 1992, I was hoisted onboard our 12-meter catamaran *Gabriel* for the first time, using my new-fangled boom extension and hoisting chair. I was trembling in fear, but all went well. With Prasert's help, I made my way into the midships cabin on my wheelchair and we set out to make *Gabriel* ready for sea. It would take a few days, and then there would have to be trials to test all the gear onboard.

I don't go on about my seaside surroundings in Thailand as I've lived all of my life on and by the sea. Rawai is my shore base, as near to my real home as I can get. I'm always aware that the rest of Thailand is close, though.

To me the sounds of waves on a beach, of the caulking of a wooden hull, or the sight of men or boys lugging a fishing net along a sandy beach, or repairing a hull, is as routine, I suppose, as the sound of road raffic or the clatter of office machinery or the sight of a television screen is to others. At my home through my window is a prospect of palm trees, a large old spreading tree, a rubber-tree plantation falling away to a sea-channel, and beyond two islands, humps of green, sometimes dark, sometimes pale, ever changing. But from the beach at Bahn Lek, I'm able to see two other islands, much farther away, dark, blue, misty and mysterious, Ko Racha Yai and Ko Racha Noi. Every single day for a year I'd stared at them from my sick-bed and promised myself that our first voyage in *Gabriel* would be to Ko Racha Yai. Since I'd lost my second leg, I'd never been away, by sea, from Phuket Island.

When I am down by our beach at Bahn Lek, in Rawai, cornered on my little terrace, I have the safety of the sea on one side, and on the other sides the rampant greenery of an unkempt tropical open space, and all the life of a tropical beach very near a marketplace; a prawn farm now, the comings and goings of men and women, boys and girls, babies; birds, cats, dogs, the theater of ordinary life ashore. When I'm onboard a boat, the safety of the sea is all around me. But my shore home is on Rawai Hill. You can't miss it—there's an anchor as big as the *QE2*'s under the eaves.

Because of fear of turning off their readers, some writers, telling a sea tale, try to disguise the maritime matter by referring, for example, to "upstairs" onboard a vessel. There's no such thing, or rather it could mean any of a dozen levels. "Left" or "right" onboard make no sense, because they change as one's position changes; they put you as the point of reference, instead of the craft. Only maritime terms will do. If you're scared off by them, try to be patient. I sympathize if you don't know the difference between "port" and "starboard," or "forward" and "aft," or if you think such terms were dreamed up by any but generations of hard-working honest mariners in the course of their often dangerous and always underpaid work, but I write of the sea, only in the language of the sea. This is for no other reason than that there is, in the English language, no other alternative. My words of being at sea are like my dog Jambo's noises: a woof of delight, a whimper of disappointment, a growl of impatience, or silence.

Stepping onboard a floating small craft is an experience like no other. It's not like entering a house, a cathedral or a museum, or boarding a plane or a train, or clambering into a car or onto a bike, a motorbike, a bus, or an army tank, come to that. It can be nothing like creeping into a space shuttle. I doubt if even stepping onboard an airship was quite the same, unless perhaps in a strong wind. The closest 20th century transport got to bestowing on us the same first-time feeling of magical mystery, or for the less intrepid, gnawing insecurity, as does boarding a sailing yacht afloat was with flying boats (amphibians). What romantic notions are conjured up by those winged wonders. Yet they were really only mostly wooden, small craft with powerful engines and wings.

It's not only the motions of a floating vessel that strikes our emotions so deeply. If it were, an elevator might give us the same sensation; imagine falling in love with a high-rise building! It's the uniqueness of each movement of a boat, the *difference* of each jiggle, each joggle, each dip and each rise, that makes boats seem human. I would have said: *that's what makes sailing the supreme sport.* But usually in sailing there are no crowds onboard, nor lines of people waiting, nor conducted tours, *yet.*

EPISODE 28

Lucks and Lacks

*Rawai beach, on the southern tip of Phuket Island in the late after-
noon. A dozen Thais, men and women, some nursing babies, stand
or sit on their haunches, on the foreshore, close to the sterns of the
catamaran-yacht* Gabriel *as she sits on the beach. Children come
and go, silently. The Thais smile as I recount my story. From time to
time, as my tale unfolds again, one-armed Som nods his head and
laughs. Loey, my captain, laughs, too, although he understands very
few English words. Prasert, our deckhand, is fast asleep.*

The bay over at the island of Ko Racha Yai—that's it, all
misty over there—is surrounded on three sides by small steep
hills. In the northwest monsoon season, the wind simply does
not reach into it. Only by craning back and watching mist
clouds streaming above can you gauge the direction and
strength of the wind in the offing. On Christmas Day morning
in 1992, there were no clouds.

The previous night we'd found that *Gabriel's* electrical
wiring was frayed, rotting and broken. I'd ordered all wires
disconnected from all batteries and appliances. Apart from a
failure of the gas stove, which had meant a cold supper, everything else had been fine.

We were up at first light and, in fitting silence, break-
fasted on cold fried fish, mangoes, and milk. Every meal with
my Thai friends is a bit like a religious observance, so much
do they respect their food and its provider.

As we ate, a large grasshopper flew over and banged into

173

the cabin door, there, just by my side, and there it hung on. I readjusted my spectacles and stared at it. It was a good three inches long and perfectly engineered. Its legs joined its body through some kind of ball-joint mechanism. Its feet were tiny sucker pads. Enlarged a thousand times it would have been a handsome horror. It was a technical marvel.

"What's that called in Thai?" I asked Loey. He was opening the deck hatch to start the outboard engine.

Loey glanced at the clinging insect. "Aharn nok," he replied. That's "bird food," see? A man of remarkable verbal economy is our Loey. I like that in a sailor, in the early morning especially.

At a silent nod from me, Som weighed our anchor, and we motored out past an anchored tour-ship. No one was on her deck. We hoisted our mainsail as we went. We could probably have safely drifted out with the tide, but I wanted to get clear of the passenger ship. No sooner had we shoved *Gabriel's* bows past the furthest outcrop of the headland when the full force of the monsoon wind and sea hit us. Boom! Like that.

Everything happened much quicker than I can tell it. Before we knew what was happening, the boat was bouncing up and down in steep seas eight feet at a rise and eight feet at a fall and . . . *Zhuttt!* . . . the bottom end of the mainsail track (on which the sail slides up the mast) had ripped out of its wooden pad on the mast. Almost at the same time . . . *Crrrkkk!* . . . the mainsail tack had torn away from the boom end. The whole mainsail, free of two of its three restraints, was now whipping around violently like a ripped circus tent in a hurricane.

Loey and Som tried to grab the mainsail, which of course was useless and to some extent dangerous. PC, the Professional Crewman who had come to us along with the yacht, appeared shocked and puzzled, and was staring as if in horror at the flogging sail.

I usually keep my voice low, as is the custom among polite people here, but in that wind and clatter, and with the seas breaking on the cliffs nearby, I had to shout. In fact, I had to holler louder than I had for years. Both Som and Loey caught the drift of my orders and hopped to it. Som ran forward to let go of the mainsail halyard, as Loey grabbed the other tiller and helped me to bring the bows into the wind. Then the mainsail shook itself, banging and clattering, down its remaining track and so down onto the deck. Som and Loey leaped on it, to dowse its flogging.

"Right, now put reefing lines (*chuat tam bye lek*) in the mainsail!" I called out to PC. Reefing points are lines which are tied to a sail's reefing points. Those are small brass eyelets which, tied down around the boom, make the sail smaller in area. I was tempted to write "luckily," but there was no luck in it; I'd had the foresight to have Loey buy and stow a reel of suitably sized line for such jobs as reefing.

Wide-eyed, PC had gaped at me. I realized that he didn't even know what a reefing line was. He had been working for years and out sailing in a boat and he never learned how to reef down the bloody mainsail! Even worse, he'd been passed to me as an experienced sailing captain who was supposed to take charge if I should have an accident or for any other reason not be able to control *Gabriel*. My breath was almost taken away. But I had to admit to myself that some of the fault lay squarely with me. On *Gabriel*'s first outward leg, the day before, I'd noticed that the reefing lines were not in the sail. I'd assumed that PC had them stowed away ready for tying on the mainsail as soon as they were needed. That was where I'd been wrong. I'd done something no skipper should ever do: I'd *assumed* instead of *ensured*.

By this time, Loey had hanked on the smallest working jib, so I could turn *Gabriel* off the wind and sail away from the threatening rocky cliffs. I had time now to look about us and realize that the wind was so strong that even with only the working jib hoisted *Gabriel* was making at least eight knots. On our leeward side—that's away from the wind—the wing-mast shrouds (they're the wire cables that hold the mast up-right) were, naturally, loose and swinging about like whips. *Zzzhhhaaanngg!*

The noise they made was terrifying to our unaccustomed ears. In a few minutes, though at the time it seemed like hours, we had the mainsail again hoisted with one reef in it, so that it was about one-third smaller. Then I laid the helm over, grabbed the monsoon wind, and off she went, like a rocket. My, oh my, how *Gabriel* goes!

I can tell you that on the homeward run to Cape Prom Thep I prayed in my teeth for our reefing points not to pull out, or the mainsail not to tear or the mast shrouds not to break, or the mast or mainsail not to go flying into the sea, but I'd no need to plead to heaven. *Gabriel* pounded home under the lee of the headland like a romping racehorse. No sooner was she under the lee and in flat water than our port rudder—the one you're sitting by, well, it's unshipped for our beach-ing, see?—anyhow, it had worked loose and had to be disconnected.

It turned out, when we later inspected the rudder, that while the pintle—that's the hinge—on the starboard rudder was of stainless steel, that of the port rudder was of ordinary steel and rusted right through.

We sailed past Nai Harn Bay, and on northwards past Kata Noi and Karon, until, in the offing of Patong Bay, a sud-den gust of wind ripped our reefed mainsail another foot or so off its mast track. I brought the boat about—that is I turned our bows through the wind—and under three reefs in the main and the working jib, headed back towards Nai Harn Bay. Then the wind dropped and against a stiff tide we made our way again past Cape Prom Thep and so into Rawai Bay here.

The sea's much rougher here at the change of season. Even as we reached in Rawai Bay, *Gabriel*'s outboard engine had stopped, as if for no reason, and five minutes later our longtail engine had suddenly packed in and left *Gabriel* rud-derless, engineless, with damaged sailing gear, the whole electrical system dead, heaving at anchor in heavy seas only a few feet off that shallow reef there, onto which, in that time of year, the seas crashed.

As the rest of our crew handed the sails, PC wanted to swim ashore but I wouldn't let him; funerals cost money. As *Gabriel* pounded up and down, up and down, I even made as if to dismount from my wheelchair to stop him. I can't quote figures, but I bet that more people have drowned trying to get ashore in rough seas over a reef than have died in boats at anchor. PC then made his way into the starboard ama, but better a live sulker than a dead starter.

Off Rawai Reef, our movement, headed as we were into the steep swells, was violent, but there was no danger of *Gabriel* being swept onto the reef—the prevailing wind, should a breeze arise at night, and the tidal current, both would head to seaward—and so we all scoffed more cold fried fish and soon Loey and Som turned in.

When tired and in doubt, the boat being safe, *turn in.*

Always be a pessimist when it comes to cruising; so I'd insisted that an oil lamp be obtained before we sailed. This Loey set in the rigging as an anchor light, in case fishing craft should come charging in during the night. It had been for Loey a long hot traipse, finding that oil lamp, but now it showed its worth.

Getting my wheelchair into the midships cabin, with Prasert steering me down the ramp, there was quite a game, but we managed it after a few bumps and clangs. I turned in thankfully, and that was our Christmas Day.

Next day's dawn was crystal-clear and calm. The sea over the reef was as flat and green as the top of a snooker table. Breakfast was fish and fried rice for the lads and porridge for me. There were no currants or sultanas onboard, but Loey had swum ashore and brought back bananas and a coconut in our dinghy *Little Legend*, and these peeled and husked were added to my porridge, so I didn't grumble.

In no time at all, the lads had the oil lamp dowsed, the boom extension on, the hangman's tackle rigged, my hoisting seat dangling, and I was lowered into *Little Legend*. With Prasert sitting in the dinghy bow, I ferried myself ashore and so up the ramp there, onto my *samlor*, and before eight o'clock I was home.

As my crew bathed themselves below, I sat quietly at my study window and looked out, across the rubber plantation, to the sea and to misty green islands on the horizon. I'd been to one of them under sail and *I'd done it for myself*. If anyone, twenty, thirty, fifty years previously, had told me that someone would one day find a way to do that, with no legs, I would have thought him crazy, and would probably have avoided his company. That for most people is their way of dealing with the unthinkable. I can't blame them, but when the unthinkable happens to them, they now perhaps have some small and humble reference.

That same day, Boxing Day, we started our refitting. For a week we were busy at it, landing both our engines ashore for complete overhaul, changing the rudder pintle, replacing the cooking stove, repairing the mainsail track, restitching and strengthening the mainsail tack, doubling all the mainsail stitching, rewiring all the electrical system. You name it—we did it. My crew also repainted the whole of *Gabriel*, topsides here and below. A white hull, but light blue otherwise. Now that you've been seeing the sun's glare all day, you can understand that nothing can be more tiring to the eyes in the tropics than the sun's reflection from white paint.

I'd obtained from Hong Kong a Magellan GPS (Global Positioning System) unit, which would provide extremely accurate navigational information besides our exact position at any time, day or night. For this unit, we fitted a permanent holder by my berth, and a remote antenna on the stern.

By New Year's Eve, *Gabriel* was like a brand-new craft. PC had sulkily departed. Som, Loey, and Prasert hoisted our working jib and, the wind blowing offshore and dead astern, *Gabriel* crossed slowly along the intricate passage, over the reef, and into deep water. There we hoisted the mainsail, and then we set off to sail the living bejasus out of *Gabriel*. As I watched our jibsail flutter aloft, I reflected that I'd never felt anything more delightful than the slow rise and fall of *Gabriel* to the scend of the sea. Sailing, except for specific moments, will never be translatable into "virtual reality." It's too emotional. It's too moody. There's always something special about someone you've sailed with, no matter who they are, no matter whether you love or hate them. You simply cannot help but feel close to them. No two sailing occasions are the same; no view for long is the same; no feeling lasts more than a fleeting moment. It's all so far from landsmen's range of experiences. For me to try to tell them of it exactly would be like attempting to describe at the same time all the colors in a shifting kaleidoscope to someone who'd been born blind.

I'd forecast that we'd push *Gabriel* to her limits, and that, in winds up to twenty-five knots, is what we did. We'd tested all our repairs, and found them good, and then as the wind slowed down we'd tested our genoa (a large jib sail) and our spinnaker sail (that's like a big balloon). More importantly, we'd also tested a few ideas on securing more safely my wheelchair.

The turn of the year saw *Gabriel* again at anchor off the island of Ko Racha Yai, and just after dawn, on New Year's Day 1993, we were sailing at full speed north to Patong Bay, then southwest out to sea, then east again on a close reach, all the way to Ao Chalong, then south again until we were almost in the lee of Ko Phi Phi, and so home to Rawai. By the GPS, in eleven hours we sailed *one hundred and eleven miles.*

What can I say about sailing at speed on a sunny day in the tropics? That the sea water was blue and green and sparkling and wonderful? That the islands and mountains around us were green and gray, shy and bold, and came closer and faded away as if by magic, and the beaches were there, then not there, clean and pure and white or a turquoise or ultramarine streak underlining a half-hidden peak? For me to tell about these things is the same as for "land-travel" authors to write about the air they breathe as they hop from airport lounge to airport lounge, and from plane to taxi.

Off the headland of Laem Kanoi, a sea eagle, pale golden, gleamed in the low late-afternoon sun. He flew over to inspect us from way above, and as *Gabriel* charged forward at full pelt, he decided to join in the fun. He dived down ahead of us a dozen times or more, and zoomed up again to the heights of a marvelous sky. Once or twice he aimed himself straight down to within inches of our masthead, then soared up a hundred yards and more straight up into the God-given heights. Then, in those moments of utter ecstasy, he and *Gabriel*, silently, with no noise but the sound of the wind on our sails and the sea's insistent slap-slap on our hulls, expressed, in their very movements, the joy of life.

I was not at all surprised; I knew that sea eagle. It was the same bird that I'd watched from my window almost every day when I'd been house-bound for months. It was the same one whose nest was in the rubber plantation between my house and the sea.

For me and my crew, these New Year sailing-trials were passages of learning and discovery. I found that I and all three of our men were bred-in-the-bone *sailors*. All that I needed to explain to them were the mechanics of *things*. The forces of the wind and the sea, for them, needed no explanation. It's as though we all had race-memory from our seafaring ancestors.

For me, as the sea eagle dived and soared, it was joy and deliverance. That sea eagle and I shared a celestial joke. "What is life about?" he seemed to be crying, "This!"

Now we could prepare *Gabriel* for a longer voyage. In all respects we were ready, except for lack of three vital things. A depthsounder we could live without, although it would be handy to see the depths at a glance instead of sounding with a line, as I had taught our Thais. Their own method was simple: look at the color of the water. But then they see things I don't.

Our first serious lack was a sailing permit for the Andaman Islands. The Indian Government had sent no reply to my applications for permission to sail in the waters of the Andaman Islands. I was reluctant to go into an area where a crew without the necessary papers might be thrown into jail.

The second serious lack was *radios*. I was wary of heading south into Malaysian or Indonesian waters without them. The risk of piracy was not great, but for sailors who are more vulnerable, it needed only one occasion . . .

The third serious lack was of a passport for Prasert. I'd figured I needed a crew of three walkers, besides Som. But getting a passport for Prasert, born of humble parents, who were now separated, would not be easy.

We—or rather I—set to, to *lick these lacks*. But first let's take a peek at my real log . . .

EPISODE 29

Log of *Gabriel*'s First Trials

Sun. Dec. 6, 1992. Took over yacht and renamed her *Gabriel*. Appointed M ("professional captain" recommended by former owner) as skipper. Mek deckhand. Neaped at Vichid Beach. Tested boom, hoisting me into cockpit. Mr. Y. Kobayashi of Yanmar Co. onboard to dinner, exactly one year after I invited him from my "death bed." New Thai ensign.

Mon. Dec. 7. 9 P.M. Unstranded, motored to Rawai beach, and careened bows-on at Bahn Lek. Slept onboard; uncomfortable: dining-table seat narrow and can't yet get down into amas.

Tues. Dec. 8. Landed loose gear into Bahn Lek. New sunshade.

Wed. Dec. 9. Tested chair hoist from beach.

Thurs. Dec. 10. Carpenters made new bridgedeck over cockpit well from 1/2-inch marine ply and hardwood. Also wheelchair ramp into main cabin. Sailmaker inspected sails. Took jib for new rivets in tack. Took on Ali as hand.

Fri. Dec. 11. 9 A.M. Final payment on yacht made. Cleaned and antifouled both ama hulls. Cleaned and painted three cans white below deck levels forward. Designed steel hoisting cage.

Sat. Dec. 12. NE 1-2. Shifted around to stern-on beach. Carpenters all afternoon on owner's forward cupboard. Ordered new companionway boards. Cleaned, painted below deck level aft and small dinghy. Appointed Pan agent. Paul arranged berth mattress with Julie. Asked arrange radio, VHF,

SSB, speedo, shock-cords, etc. also electrician for check. From Phuket ordered 12 T-shirts, one for Mike.

Sun. Dec. 13. NE 1-2. Prasert off. Carpenters: cupboard, main door, midships cabin, food cupboard in starboard ama. Khun Ith, lawyer, took ship's papers to re-register, also copy charter agreement. Ith to call Tuesday. Taught Ali, Loey, Mek simple knots. Jib-sail returned.

Mon. Dec. 14. NE 2-4. Companionway and ama food-lockers. Fitting bigger anchoring cleats. Montri, Sac, to Pkt in afternoon shopping for gear. Loey repairing watertank in house. Longtail prop ashore for replacement & spare. (Paul.)

Tues. Dec. 15. NE 2-4. Lawyer Khun Ith came. M must go to Chachasao to transfer registration ("move the soul") to Phuket! Once done, I "can officially own boat!!" Carpenter finished big jobs. Fitted plastic fender around *Little Legend*. Stainless steel hoisting chair (cage) completed.

Wed. Dec. 16. NE 1-2. Adapted *Little Legend* dinghy to fit hoisting chair. Was hoisted aboard in new cage. Success. Surveyed work to date. Fixed GPS, Radio, VHF stowages, etc. Montri and Loey to Ayutthaya (about 600 miles) for registration transfer. Expect them back on Saturday, with charts, tide-tables, fenders, talcum, etc. Epoxied bridgedeck board. Everything to plan and so far on time.

Thurs. Dec. 17. NE 1-2. Last night, Mek (without leave) had motorcycle accident carrying a passenger. Mek badly bruised on left foot and leg, passenger head injuries reported serious. Mek at hospital. Ali Mate. Work onboard curtailed. Guarding *Gabriel*. Phone line down.

Fri. Dec. 18. NE 2-4. Ali epoxied deck board. Awaiting news of Mek's injured friend and the return of Montri and Loey.

Sat. Dec. 19. ENE 2. Mek's friend not fractured. Loey and M arrived A.M.: all well. *Gabriel* now legally in Phuket; hoisted all three foresails for six *makee-learners*. Concrete sections delivered for Bahn Lek watertank.

Sun. Dec. 20. NE 1-2. Carpenter: nav table, crew started

small dinghy gunwale. Designated chair-holding ring-bolts. Taught Ali whip fender lanyards with fishing line. Phone line: faxed Mr. L.C. Morgan, Vice-Consul, U.K. Embassy from Rawai Plaza, to lean on the telephone authority.

Mon. Dec. 21. NE 0-1. To Ao Markham. Port Captain in Bangkok. "Technician" to inspect *Gabriel* "tomorrow." Bought 120-amp battery, breaker, and fuses. Montri's heel-stitches removed. 12-volt adapter not included in GPS kit; faxed to AVT Bangkok (agent) for unit.

Tues. Dec. 22. NE 0-1. Phone line "down" five days. Mek, Loey to TOT; again faxed Brit. Embassy. M, Ali preparing paintwork topsides. Som: Enablement water-tank. Lack of phone line very frustrating. At 11 A.M. I went to TOT myself, with Prasert and Loey. Technicians came and restored line 2 P.M. Exhausted. No sign of Port Captain's "technician."

Wed. Dec. 23. NE 0-1. In A.M. to Port Captain's Office with M and Loey. M has tire puncture. Mr. Vichet says I can't be owner of Thai-registered vessel as I don't own land . . . I can't own land as I'm not Thai, nor married to one. I nominate Loey as the "Thai owner." Tested boom-extension. Marked out GPS system in cabin. Loey signed to me a lifetime charter. New name on stern. Som making forward tank for Bahn Lek and new dinghy gunwale. PC and Loey to Port Captain's office in P.M. to clinch sale which they later say will "take a month!"

Thurs. Dec. 24. NE 3-0. 0900. To *Gabriel*, weighed and sail trials with main, jib, and genoa. A lively , fast boat, but with much to be sorted out. Midship deck pounds in swells. Very fast in flat, calm seas, making 12-15+ knots. Somehow I know this is the fastest she has ever sailed. M confirms this. Out towards Ko Racha and back to Nai Harn, where stood off, then sailed for Ko Racha until wind dropped. 9 hp longtail-engine overheated, 25 hp outboard races. To anchor off Rawai. 30 miles est. A lively chop when wind is against incoming tide. Sail trials a success.

Fri. Dec. 25. NE 3-1. Both yacht engines dead. Montri shipped LL dinghy 6 hp, motored into Rawai Beach, removed rudders, turned bows out. Both engines landed. Applied by fax to RNSA for British registry.

Sat. Dec. 26. Outboard fitted new propeller. Longtail engine to Phuket for check/overhaul. Preparing topsides for painting. Building watertank ashore at Enablement. Preparing pix for release. Must delay voyage departure until engine returns. Aiming for Jan. 15.

Sun. Dec. 27. Cleaning topsides for painting.

Mon. Dec. 28. Ditto. Photos.

Tues. Dec. 29. First coat light blue topsides.

Wed. Dec. 30. Mek fired drunk. Second coat light blue topsides.

Thurs. Dec. 31.1500. Motored to offing, hoisted main and jib. Took photos. Course to Ko Racha Yai. Wind failed at 1600; motored to anchorage with Yanmar longtail. *Andaman Princess* had dropped hundreds of Japanese on beach. Quiet evening and night, although sailing to anchor.

Fri. Jan. 1, 1993. NE 4-5. 0730. Weighed. Hoisted main & jib. *Gabriel* dropped off a sea, mainsail tack track ripped out of the boom. Tied down tack, put in a reef in main. Made Prom Thep in 1.25 hours (about 8.5 knots). Off Patong Bay at about 1030, a sudden blast of wind ripped out the mainsail track bottom section. Put in two reefs, but after hard beating to windward, motored into anchorage at 1230. Very noisy from jet-skis. At 1600, wind ENE gusting to 5, weighed, course under genoa, then 3-reefed main, for Nai Harn, where motored in at 1800 and anchored. Electrics not working. No lights, no fan. Som went overland to Rawai and brought us food in his longtail! About 60 miles.

Sat. Jan. 2. Under power to Rawai. Off Prom Thep, starboard rudder failed at pintle. We have found weak spots which are always present in second-hand yacht. In stiff chop, I was off-loaded into *Little Legend* (half-terrified) and landed at 0900. *Gabriel* brought into Rawai beach in P.M. M & Li. 5 miles.

Sun. Jan. 3. Rudders off, scraped and cleaned. S.S. reinforcements made.

Mon. Jan. 4. Mast-tracks plugged and re-fixed. Rudders repaired. Completed small dinghy re-build. Electrician replacing all old wiring and relocating batteries.

Tues. Jan. 5. Checked masthead light & replaced. GPS wiring completed; antenna fixed on coachroof. Cleaning paint off deck-boards. Photos shot Dec 31 no good as film did not advance.

Wed. Jan. 6 to Sun. 10. I had chest cold. Routines onboard.

Sun. Jan. 10. Onboard at 0930. Weighed at 0930. Engine trials. Under both Yamaha and Yanmar to Ban Nip. Hoisted genoa. Sailed to Rawai for pictures. Down genoa, up spinnaker. Back in as tide drops at 1430. 10 miles.

Mon. Jan. 11. Fixed GPS antenna on stern-pole. Sending pix.

Tues. Jan. 12. Traced and restored 12V to GPS system. *Gabriel* is to be on cover of *Multihulls* magazine. Discussing film with Patrick Cusick.

Wed. Jan. 13. Bilge pump fitted. Sent off pix to U.S. donors. Viewed video of *Little Legend as* shown in Australia.

Thurs. Jan. 14. Fitted anchor block. Cleaning furniture for varnish. Pix to selected donors.

Sun. Feb. 7. Out for two hours' practice with Som as skipper, Loey, and Ali.

Reveries

While I'd been afloat in *Gabriel* on trials and for filming, our house at Rawai Hill had been illegally entered into. The news was broken to me by the film producer, Patrick Cusick.

My first thought was that thieving goes on everywhere. My second thought was for my journal. I've never had many belongings, apart from boat gear, and there were not many in my home anyway, but what if the house breaker, in his frustration at not finding much else of value, were to burn our house down, or steal my old computer, or fling my journal and files about? I couldn't bite my nails; the first rule in the tropics is to always keep them very short.

"He not do anything stupid," Som had replied when I blurted my dread to him. "He only want money."

My next thoughts were how to get myself ashore. It was late afternoon and the tide was out, so sailing *Gabriel* round to Rawai and using *Little Legend* to get ashore was out of the question; over Rawai reef there would not be enough water even for *Little Legend*, and she draws only three inches. The wind had dropped anyway, and it would have been a slow job to motor round to Rawai.

"We go into Nai Harn beach and Loey and I take you ashore in *Gabriel*'s dinghy," volunteered Som. Good man (except when handing out land-leases to prawn farms).

Nai Harn Beach was a mere mile or so away from us. So simple normally, but for me *frightening*. I had never, since my second leg came off, gone ashore by any other means but *Little Legend*. I'd thought about it, of course, but when it came to actually doing it, it was scary. I suppose it's like people who work in high-rise buildings and know that they might have to leave via a fireman's ladder one day, but who put the thought away.

The wind had dropped. As *Gabriel* motored, how slow she seemed, under power, even at six knots, into Nai Harn Bay and right close to the beach. Our lads prepared the boom-extension and hangman's tackle, I swung into my hoist-seat, over the side I went, and down into the bow of *Gabriel's* tender. Even though the sea was calm, the dinghy bobbed up and down alarmingly. The sea here, on the edge of the beach, was a mere three feet deep. Som and Loey jumped into the sea, but carefully, so as not to rock my dinghy. As Som and Loey waded ashore, pushing the dinghy with them, I clung to its sides, terrified of it capsizing. Prasert had set the anchor and stayed onboard *Gabriel* as anchor guard.

Curiously enough, my main fear of capsizing into the sea was not of drowning, (a non-swimmer, I had two good men with me) but of wetting my right stump sore. It was salutary for an old salt to be reminded of how landlubbers feel when they first go afloat.

Although there was not a breath of wind, the sea-swell surge on Nai Harn Beach suddenly heaved up my dinghy and threw it right up the beach about twenty yards. I've no idea how Loey and Som managed to hold on, and keep the dinghy upright and at right angles to the shoreline, but somehow they did. The beach end where we washed up was almost empty of sunbathers, but we managed to be cast ashore on dry sand right beside a heavy man sitting on a deck chair under a beach parasol. He wore dark glasses and very little else. He must have been around forty-five or so. He nodded to me and wished us courteously "Gut afternoon." His accent was German. His cool greeting restored my flagging faith in the future of Europe.

As Loey and Som, one on each side, picked me up in my hoist-seat and started to carry me the fifty yards or so through fine, powdery, blazing hot sand towards the relief of shade, I nodded back at the tourist. I wondered how he knew I was English-speaking, and at the Dali-esque incongruity of us and him together on an empty beach. It seemed to me that to him the appearance, from out of the sea, of what appeared to be a legless old man sitting in a steel cage, being lugged around by two young, but by this time rather savage-looking sun-black men, was the most normal thing in the world, but that's the way it was.

I was not astonished at all when we reached shade, to find it was within yards of my sanctuary rock, at the base of the small wooded cliff. This is where I'd first resolved to get myself back afloat, and returning here was yet another sign, to me, that what I had done, making an idle day dream come true, had all been part of an immutable design.

Right, close to my sanctuary rock, I was in my stainless-steel hoisting cage set on hard ground, upright on my stumps at the height of a three-year old child, wincing with stress, in hot, dead air, badly missing the protecting pretense of my dog Jambo—though he wouldn't harm a flea—glancing around nervously in case a snake slithered through the long grasses all around me, under the tree shade on a rough track above the now-deserted Nai Harn Beach.

Loey had disappeared down the track in the direction of the very posh Yacht Club Hotel to raise a taxi or a tuk-tuk, while Som had started back down the beach to swim to *Gabriel*.

Even as our lads left me feeling utterly weak and vulnerable and alone, I thanked God that I *was* alone. Ridicule needs more than one person. Not to have an audience was worth almost any risk. I cursed for not having had the foresight to bring along a hammer, so I might flatten a threatening snake, or a knife or cutlass to kill it. There's not much room for green thoughts when you're all alone on the ground, immobile except for balancing on your hands and with the prospect of dragging your ass along at the rate of about one mile a week. On the other hand, it doesn't do to dwell too much on your fears and isolation, even when you know your home has been broken into. If there's nothing for you to do, then do it with enthusiasm.

I glanced across the man-made lagoon. Sunlight glittered from it in golden flakes. There was nothing I could do. It would be pointless to worry about the snakes. I lit a cigarette, stared out to sea and watched the sunset. There was small chance that snakes would be out and about at the end of the dry season. If you have to worry, see a tropical sunset first.

It was all amazing. The whole world before me, the huge sweep of Nai Harn Bay and its surrounding mountains and sea, was now a blaze of cooling color. The sun had scarcely set when the western principality of the sky became pink, then rose, then ruby red. The undersides of the few thin clouds radiated like fire across the sky. Mozart's music was depicted in a blaze of glory. The topsides of the clouds in contrast were a deep Wagnerian valley of charcoal-black. It looked as if the entire sky had caught aflame. The scene lasted a full five minutes before it faded. The glow went out in the uppermost clouds, like a light switched off, then the lower clouds darkened and the horizon dimmed as the color burned away, leaving the sky ashen-gray with streaks of charcoal here and there. I understood now why so many Asian tourists made for Prom Thep, to stand in silent crowds atop the headland and watch the sunsets. I understood better how Beethoven could write his Ninth Symphony while he had been as deaf as a doorknob.

I stared at the sea again and at the changing colors as the daylight faded over Nai Harn Bay. As the color of the sand changed from orange to silver, and the hills around from green to gray and black, I saw sturdy, beautiful, well-educated sea people of the future. They would know of sciences and materials and powers beyond our imagining. They would build graceful sailing craft, bigger and stronger and faster than anything we now know, that could be submerged in the ocean in rough weather, so they might wait out storms in the still and safe comfort of the depths. They would build craft that will reach to the very bottom of the deeps, miles below the changing surface of the ocean, deeper than the summit of Mount Everest is high, where wonders exist of which we now know nothing, where they might find the relics of their predecessors. There, in the almost unimaginable depths, they would mine precious metals and materials and extract great wealth to the deprivation of nobody and the gain of all. The sea people would be at one with all the creatures of the deep, and learn from them, and live with them in peace and harmony. They would join their craft together underwater, and before children I am seeing now die of old age, they might form a city in the deeps, a city vast enough for greenery, but silent except for the low sweet tones of music . . . And moveable city could join onto moveable city, and cities as big as London or New York would come and go with creatures and fabulous forms of life onboard, and clusters of cities, themselves all moving together through the still depths of the oceans as one, to form a nation, or solitary ships, making their own way or keeping their own station, as the people in them pleased . . .

And the name of one of those vast, silent, safe, clean nations in the oceans of planet Earth would be *Atlantis*.

They'd also probably have house breakers.

I laughed and that woke me from my daydream. There was no sound, except for the sea. I was sleepy. I could not doze off here above Nai Harn Beach, alone in the open; I would have to stop daydreaming and exercise my memory.

I thought of other colors in nature, and recalled the names of some of fellow sea denizens—dozens of them. I needed no encyclopedia, nor dictionary: yellow jack, goatfish, scarlet and

gold butterfly fish, blood and red-gold and blue gobies, duck-
egg-blue parrot fish, deep bronze cobia, batfish the same color,
black spotted flying gurnard, scarlet hogfish, zoophytes a
hundred different colors; and the plant life—what wonders!—
beige gulfweed, dark-green laminaria, brilliant emerald sea-
lettuce, red, gold and amber fucus, algae weed the same
colors, orange carrageen, puce Ceylon-moss, and rich bladder-
kelp; and shells: razor clam, long-horned scapapoda, azure
sea snails, delicately-spotted olive-shells, golden-green chi-
tons, spirally wentletraps, great golden cowries up to two feet
long, leopard-colored volutes, deep-black abalones, thorny
oysters and lovely yellow-to-golden-to-brown purple tellin
bivalves. And the birds, the lovely birds of the sea: black
guillemots, double-crested cormorants, gray shearwaters,
terns, eider-ducks, emerald-sheen-headed mallards, sea ea-
gles, garnets, gulls, frigate birds, and wide wing-spreaded albatross over the Southern Ocean . . . With the memories of
these for company, what old sailor need fall asleep when he
should be wide awake, or ever feel sorry for himself or be
lonely?

Who, I asked myself, in such a place as this, by the sanctuary rock, nestled close to the very breast of Mother Earth
and seeing all the marvels of the western sky, in bright day
and dark night, could ever be seriously cynical or callous?

My reverie was broken by the sudden noise of a familiar-
sounding motorcycle engine. I turned to look in the direction
of the purr. In the gloaming, the bright yellow of my sidecar
came bumping through the grass between the tracks. It was
Som's younger brother, Nuey, very quick witted he is. In my
sidecar, Jambo wagged his tail and I grinned because I knew I
was once again safe from snakes.

Nuey had heard of the house breaking and that *Gabriel*
had anchored in Nai Harn Bay, and had surmised I would not
be able to get ashore in Rawai, and would be coming ashore
elsewhere to try to get home quickly. I made up my mind

never again to underestimate the Thai "bush-telegraph" and the intelligence of boys of thirteen. I thanked Nuey and made a silent promise to pay him for his trouble and thoughtfulness. I hailed Loey, who had turned up with Nuey, to lift me onto my motorbike, and I was back in control of myself.

Loey had turned up with a borrowed motorcycle and went ahead to my house. I called off at Bahn Lek, where Jambo still awaited me, mooning at *Little Legend*'s launching track.

By the time I got home, Loey had switched off the alarm system. The house breaker had staved in the kitchen door, breaking the alarm circuit, and the loud noise of the alarm bell had evidently frightened him off right away, for nothing at all was missing. My journal, half a lifetime of hard, painful labor, hours and hours of it at two pages a day, was safe.

I reflected on how, if it had not been for the film makers— such comings and goings and ooh-ing and ahh-ing, and do this and that and do it again, please—only a very few people would have known we were off to sea. As it was, everyone in and around Rawai knew, including any house breakers. Everyone had known that I was off to sea with all my crew, and would be out all day, if not two or three days. It was the first break-in ever reported in our area. So it seemed to me that the very presence of film cameras for any reason encourages outrages.

During *Gabriel*'s coming cruise, our house would need a guard while we were away at sea, and I simply did not have enough money to pay one. Neither did I have enough to take on an extra hand for *Gabriel*, and in any case it takes time to train a crewman, especially in my circumstances. Prasert would guard ashore, and as in *Gabriel* we'd be short handed, we'd have to reduce our range for the cruise.

Epilogue:
Harking Back

Long, long ago, a small boy lugged a sea-bag—almost as big as himself—in the sunshine of an early spring morning along a jetty overshadowed by the tall masts of working sailing barges. Time and again he dodged behind, to him, huge bollards to avoid being knocked down by great cart-horses hauling wagon-loads of cargo to and from the ships.

There were no romantic dreams in that small boy's mind. After a two-day steam-train-slog from the purple shore of West Wales to the green county of Kent, all he dreamed of was breakfast and sleep . . . he had no inkling—none at all—of what lay before him. The chances are, I suspect, that if he had known of the wonders ahead, he would have walked a little faster; if he had known of the disasters—a little slower; but boys, fortunately for them, know of neither.

Fifty-six years ago last May . . . Sometimes the memory of that walk flashes in my mind, and then it seems that the small boy was not really me, but someone else entirely; a moment's reflection tells me that this is true. We constantly renew ourselves; our cells regenerate. No one is more than seven years old perhaps, after all. For certain, no one is seventy, not even I.

In the next sixteen months, before we went to war with Hitler's menace, I lived a life that I suppose many boys dreamed of—sailing across the English Channel to France (*"You can't go ashore in France, Nipper; the blokes wear scent and play football on Sundays!*") and the Channel Islands in the winter and to Holland and Germany in the summers. It is said that we recall only pleasant memories, and I suppose that's true; I have to force myself to recall all the back-breaking labor, the cold, the wet, hauling in two-ton anchors by hand-capstan, storms, my hands skinned to the bone after chucking or stacking 10,000 house bricks in a day's cargo loading. Gloves were for gentlemen's chauffeurs—no deckie-boy would be seen dead in them.

In my first ship, *Second Apprentice*, my skipper was Tansy Lee, 86 years of age, his only books the Bible and the manifest. Bert the Mate's sole ambition was to tend a garden. Ted, the Third Hand, fifteen then, had been dredged out of some London orphanage. Ted's fantasies of himself as a soccer star—in ripe Cockney, ashore or afloat—would have made Gazzer dizzy.

The Luftwaffe sunk *Second Apprentice* in mid-'41, and all three of them died—along with my replacement, whom I glimpsed only briefly: another snot-nosed graduate of a Home for Orphan Boys. When he joined the ship, the sole of his left shoe was dangling, so it looked like his foot was laughing. I don't recall his name—only his laughing shoe.

The deaths of my first real mates, and wanting to clobber someone for it, was, I think, what kept me going onboard His Majesty's destroyers, and not much let-up ashore, especially in Chatham Barracks.

But nothing lasts for ever; the war ended, somehow, and the six years that followed until '51 were, I suppose, the gravy-days of my navy-days, cruising on exotic shores, loitering in esoteric bars and hoisting my gaff with erotic ferocity. "Showing the flag," we called it, then.

Looking back, my early small craft voyages were—although of course we didn't realize it then—much more difficult than in these days. For one thing, most hulls were wooden, and by the time we'd voyaged from say Holland to

Brazil, we could practically hear the teredo worms spitting out the nails as they chewed up the planking. There were no such thing as marinas then; we used to careen the boat on some calm beach and burn the worms out with a blow torch. Some of them would be up to ten feet long and thick as your wrist. A Dutchman I knew used to eat them.

No satellite navigators, no Loran, either. If you didn't get your sextant shots and sums fairly right, you might wind up anywhere from Antarctica to Florida instead of Brazil . . . We became dead-reckoning machines. In a pub, I would know if the toilet was NNW of the public bar . . . I would know, without glancing outside the door, the wind speed and direction, even with six pints under my belt. We learned what we could of celestial navigation from other delivery skippers and what was missing we improvised on until we somehow got it as near to right as we might guess. We didn't encounter many professional navigators, apart from certain night-ladies who might be honored with the title, but when we did, they seemed to either think of us "delivery skippers" and "cruising men" as equals in skill or—more often—dead lucky. The few navigational "experts" who had taken to small craft that I myself got to know fairly well, almost all, to my recollection, ended up in some kind of disaster caused by faulty gear or seamanship—or just bad luck. It seemed to us that in small craft, good gear, good seamanship, good navigation, and good luck rarely went together. It was ten years before I ever had a proper navigation table to plot on. Before that, it had either been the steeply-heeling, jerky saloon table or the top of a wet biscuit tin.

The only self-draining cockpits or mechanical mainsail-reefing gear I ever saw, before the end of the '50s, were in elderly Bristol Channel pilot cutters. The early wind-vane steerers were complicated, intricate, feeble jokes, and about as dependable as the average small-craft diesel engine in those days, which meant there was a 25 percent chance, if you were lucky, that it might work when you really needed it.

Sails were of canvas, which meant that unless you cosseted them carefully they would fall to pieces, under the tropical sun and rain, very swiftly.

Radar was something mysterious that revolved atop ship's masts. We knew it had something to do with navigation, but weren't ever quite sure what. Radio transmitters in small craft were unheard of. Refrigeration was something that people like Errol Flynn or Lady Astor had onboard their luxury yachts. Our hot water and food were boiled—in fair weather—in a pan on a kerosene or coal stove or lugged from the nearest pub. In hard blows, it was grab a tin, open it, chuck the contents in a pan and boil it. Scoff it out of the pan, too. But many's the time I would have bet Escoffier's renderings could taste no better.

Now there are, at least on the coasts of advanced countries, amenities like marinas with showers and electricity and even telephones laid on, and running fresh water, restaurants and garbage bins . . . There's no doubt about it. With all the modern facilities and gadgets, yacht voyaging must be a thousand percent easier and more comfortable now than it was in the '50s. But allow an old sailor a little grouch.

The sailing people I met in those years—I never heard the term "yachtie" until about '72. A kaleidescopic procession passes before my mind's eye: the ancient, the babies, the weirdos, the steadies, the false, the true, the proud, the pitiful, the drunk, the sober, the stoned, the religious, the sacrilegious . . . the Swedish hermit who'd been anchored off the coast of Venezuela for eight years—the bottom of his boat looked like the Hanging Gardens of Babylon; Bill Tilman in *Mischief* (greatest of them all) on the coast of Iceland—little idea where he was, even at anchor—scoffing yogurt by the bucketful; Henry Gilmore pretending to be stone-deaf every time a customs officer came onboard his boat *Bill Adams*; Bernard Moitessier lecturing me for hours on the perils of fostering ulcers with alcohol, and him with a cupboard full of ulcer pills onboard *Joshua*; Ronnie the Swiss fire-eater, who took off across the Atlantic navigating on a school atlas (he was never heard of again); Edward Alcard, a beauty-loving genius who practically wore a groove around Cape Horn; Jerry Malone, who was struck by lightning off New Guinea—the shock, he said, welded all 300 of his beer cans to his steel bilges so that he had to spend a week chiseling them free.

But I can't think of any of my past voyages—not even my passage down the River Danube through Communist Eastern Europe in *Outward Leg* in '85; not even my passage in '87 in the fishing boat *Henry Wagner* right through Thailand with four fellow-disabled—that have been, in the forming of it, as intricate, as problematical, as complex, as difficult or as potentially worthwhile as those I undertook in 1992 and 1993.

They weren't long voyages, but their purpose was to get me, as much as possible by my own efforts, from here, by my sick-bed, to a beach, across that beach, down to the sea, and to a distant shore under sail. That was my small challenge, with both my legs off at the thighs. That was the reason for all the rest.